How We Trade Options

Jon and Pete Najarian are professional investors, noted media analysts, and co-founders of optionMONSTER and tradeMONSTER.

Jon, the oldest of four brothers, and Pete, the youngest, grew up in California and Minnesota, each following their father in playing college football. Both would enjoy stints in the professional game before turning to another pursuit sometimes seen as a contact sport – trading on the Chicago Board Options Exchange (CBOE).

Jon, often known by his call letters, "DRJ", a nod to his dad, launched his financial career in 1981 after a concluding Mike Singletary was likely to beat him out as starting linebacker for the Chicago Bears. Jon would go on to trade in the pits for some 25 years. In 1989 he founded Mercury Trading, running the company for 15 years until 2004, when he sold his floor-trading operations to Citadel, one of the world's largest hedge funds.

Pete, who enjoyed several seasons with the Tampa Bay Buccaneers and Minnesota Vikings, took up trading in 1992. Joining his brother, he subsequently led Mercury's entry onto the New York Stock Exchange, and served as president from 2000 to 2004.

More recently the duo developed and patented trading applications used to identify unusual activity in stock, options, and futures markets, notably the Heat Seeker® program, which scans up to 7 million quotes per second.

Jon contributes to CNBC, has been published in Barron's, and is widely cited by financial media including the Wall Street Journal, Reuters, and Bloomberg. Pete is a cast member of CNBC's "Fast Money".

Founded in 2005, the tradeMONSTER Group of companies provides brokerage and trading services intended to give individual investors greater discipline and confidence, thereby narrowing the gap between self-directed and institutional investing. At www.optionmonster.com, the Chicago-based company delivers actionable trading ideas and advanced education, while also operating popular investment conferences. tradeMONSTER, at www.trademonster.com, has several times been rated by Barron's as "Best for Options Traders."

How We Trade Options

Building Wealth, Creating Income, and Reducing Risk

Jon "DRJ" & Pete Najarian

To my beautiful wife, Brigid, who lets me be a Road Monster
and gives me endless love and support, and our wonderful daughters
Tristen and Finola. To our parents, Mignette and Dr. John S. Najarian,
for their love and life lessons we carry with us every day: the respect
for people of all races, work ethic, and faith that you showed us
by how you lived your lives.

—Jon

To my wife, Loopie, and children Alexis and Kole,
who traveled across the country to keep our family as close as we are today.
Moving from the only city either of my children ever knew, at an important
time in their lives, was a sacrifice that I can repay only with my love
and commitment as an appreciative father.

—Pete

TABLE OF CONTENTS

INTRODUCTION

After finishing my first book about options amid the dot-com collapse in 2001, I assumed that I would never get another opportunity to write about the markets in turmoil of such magnitude. Little did I know that we would witness far more sweeping changes to our financial system and everyday trading barely a decade later. To that end, I recruited my brother Pete to help map this drastically changed landscape.

The earlier crisis introduced the general public to the concept of stock options, as an entire generation of dot-com entrepreneurs and employees learned how these contracts worked within their companies. Whether these internal options translated into stakes worth millions or nothing, it was an indelible lesson.

Thanks to the entrepreneurial culture of Silicon Valley, terms such as "vesting," "grants," and "strike prices" became part of the nomenclature for twentysomethings who might otherwise never have owned a single share in any company. That, in turn, helped spur interest in trading of stock options on the open market.

At the same time, the explosion of online brokerages, social networks, and vast amounts of free research on the web initiated millions of "retail" investors who could venture into the trading world on their own. If that planted the seeds of interest, the financial crisis of 2008 watered the phenomenon of option trading into full bloom.

For generations, Wall Street has been dominated by monolithic institutions that reserved the most lucrative opportunities for members of their exclusive domain. Wielding dominant influence and operating behind the scenes, these powerful entities—investment banks, hedge funds, large brokerages, and other "masters of the universe"—effectively squeezed out countless traders who simply couldn't compete against the enormous positions taken on a daily, if not hourly, basis.

All that changed when the mortgage industry crashed. The massive disruption that ensued shook markets around the globe and ended a Wall Street hegemony that had reigned for more than 100 years. As with many natural and man-made catastrophes throughout history, however, what initially considered scorched earth quickly became viewed as a level playing field.

In this new world order, achieving returns comparable to those of professionals does not require huge amounts of capital or expertise in obscure vehicles such as credit-default swaps. But it does demand mastery of a newer products, strategies, and technologies.

The cataclysm has not only fundamentally altered the financial universe but, coming so soon after the dot-com crash, has also made clear the imperative for retailers to take decision-making into their own hands with such tools as derivative stock options. In chaos, as it's been said, is opportunity.

— **Jon Najarian**

PART ONE:
How We Trade Options

NOT THE OLDEST PROFESSION, BUT CLOSE

So what exactly is a stock option? There are a number of ways to answer that question, but let's start with term itself: It is a contract that gives you the option to trade a stock. You might ask why anyone would want to do something like this, which probably sounds mind-numbingly boring on its face. But you might be equally interested to know that the answer is rooted in a colorful history that some scholars date back to ancient Greece.

Thales of Miletus is credited with conceiving the notion in addressing the needs of the olive market. Though best known as a father of Greek philosophy, Thales was also a shrewd entrepreneur who keenly understood the dynamics of supply and demand. And in the Mediterranean around 600 B.C., few commodities were in as much demand as olives.

One year, while anticipating a particularly bountiful harvest thanks to good weather, Thales supposedly paid a fee to reserve the use of olive presses throughout the coastal city of Miletus that season—cornering the market in the process. This made Miletus an early option trader, if not the first. He could have tried to rent the presses after the trees bore fruit much later, but then he would be competing with droves of other merchants. Instead, like a modern-day trader, he purchased the right to use the presses rather than buy them outright—thereby ensuring the ability to participate in a big harvest but limiting his risk in case the forecast proved wrong.

The experience is akin to a trader who buys an option in a stock that he hopes will rise with some future event, such as a new product or quarterly earnings report. It also highlights another major reason that traders use options: to manage risk. When you purchase stock, by contrast, you risk losing the entire amount of those shares if it collapses; but when you purchase an option to buy that stock, at only a fraction of the share price, you can choose not to exercise it and therefore avoid the huge losses.

Perhaps most important, Miletus gave birth to a concept that has become known in the investment world as a derivative—a financial instrument that can profit from an asset but without necessarily owning it. Historians believe that the first exchange based on such derivatives was created in 18th-century Japan. The Dojima Exchange was established in the 1730s to allow futures trading in rice, an effort to avoid wild fluctuations in the price of the country's grain staple. Merchants could lock in prices well ahead of harvesting season to stabilize the market. Eventually the concept spread to futures trading in all manner of commodities, from potatoes and butter to oil and gold. But options were initially used only for trading stock in companies.

So let's fast-forward a few thousand years to discuss the concept of options in modern markets. Most of you probably understand the basics of trading stocks: You buy shares in a company, hope that the price rises, then at some point sell it at a profit or a loss. You pay the full face value up front, whatever the market is asking at the time. And once you have made the purchase, there's no going back.

An option, however, is exactly what its name implies: It is a contract that allows you to buy or sell something. You are paying for the right to trade shares, but it does not necessarily obligate you to do so. Why is that appealing? It gives you flexibility. And that flexibility can be a huge advantage in a marketplace where the odds often seem stacked against the individual investor.

Suppose you hear about some premium cigars for sale a good price—let's call them pre-embargo Cubans, to make things interesting (and legal). You want to buy some, but you're not sure if they're authentic. The quoted price is $100 apiece, which is steep but still fair because they will undoubtedly go up in value if they're real.

You could take a chance and buy them at full price, but if they're counterfeit you will lose most if not all of your $100 investment. But what if you paid a nominal amount—say, $2—for the right to buy these cigars, dependent on whether they are authenticated? If they are bogus, you will have lost the $2, but that's a lot better than having paid $100 up front. If they are real, you can buy them for $102—which is $2 more than the face value, but doesn't that seem like a small price to make sure that your investment was safe?

The same premise applies to stock options. In the case of buying a call, which is the most common way that traders use options to purchase stock, you pay a relatively small premium for the right to own shares.

For instance, suppose you want to buy 300 shares of Company X, which are going for $100 apiece. The company is scheduled to report quarterly earnings in a month, and you think that the stock will go a lot higher after that. Yet, as with all things in life, nothing is certain: Everyone thought the same thing in the last quarter, but the earnings turned out to be awful and the stock tanked.

So instead of buying the shares outright, you buy the option to purchase them. Just as you did with the cigars, you paid $2 for the right to buy the stock at $100 apiece. There's one important difference, however: Each option contract controls 100 shares. That means 1 call cost $200 in this case, for the option to buy 100 shares at $100 each. Because you want to buy 300 shares, you will need to buy 3 calls for a total cost of $600.

But if the company reports strong earnings and shares go through the roof, you will have locked in the purchase price of the stock and will be able to sell it for a lot more money.

> **Scenario 1:** Company X does indeed beat forecasts by Wall Street analysts, and its stock jumps to $122. The $2 calls you bought locked in your entry purchase price at $100 per share, so you have a profit of $20 per share for 100 shares. Your 3 calls cost $600 for the right to buy 300 shares at $100 apiece, or $30,000. Those shares are now worth $36,600, so you are up $6,000 ($36,600 - $30,000 entry price - $600 for 3 calls = $6,000).

> **Scenario 2:** Company X issues another lousy report, sending the stock into a tailspin down to $70 per share. If you had bought 300 shares outright at $100 apiece for a total of $30,000, you would be down $9,000 ($30,000 - 300 shares x $70). But you paid only $600 for the option, not the obligation, to buy those shares, which you obviously won't do now because they're worth much less than your pre-determined "strike price" of $100. That $600 is your total loss, which is a lot less painful than $9,000.

Even better, those Cohibas did in fact turn out to be the real deal, and they've doubled in value since you bought them. So the $2 you paid for the option in that case seems like nothing now, right? In all of these cases, you can see where the use of options might limit profits but also limits risk.

There are also option strategies that can be used in conjunction with existing stock positions. In fact, the most popular option trade is known as a "covered call," in which an investor sells options to make some additional income while holding onto stock. This strategy is typically used when an investor believes that a stock will trade sideways or might even fall in the near term but will eventually rise, so he or she does not want to sell the shares just yet.

In this trade, calls are sold at a designated strike price and contract duration that the investor believes won't be reached before they expire. This allows him or her to collect the premium from the sale of those options while hanging onto the stock. You might have heard us refer to this strategy as "getting paid to wait" for the shares to rally.

> **Example:** You decided to exercise those 3 calls you bought earlier in Company X, so you now own 300 shares with the stock trading at $122. Because those surprisingly strong earnings drove up the stock price, there's a lot of speculation that it will go even higher. That has boosted call premiums to levels that you, who have been watching this stock for months if not years, believe are way too high.

In fact, you notice that some March 150 calls are going for $2.50, meaning that some traders are buying those calls in the belief that the stock will rise past $150 by the time those contracts expire in mid-March. But it's already late January, and you highly doubt that that Company X will go from $122 to $150—a 23 gain—in less than two months without any other earnings reports or other catalysts to move the share price.

So you decide to sell 3 calls at that $2.50 premium, for a tidy sum of $750 (3 calls x 100 shares x $2.50 premium). If the stock does rally above $150 by mid-March, you will be forced to sell your 300 shares at that price and miss out on any further gains beyond that strike price. But if Company X stays below $150, you will collect that $750 as profit while those calls expire worthless and you keep the stock.

The two trades outlined above—buying the calls before you own the stock, then selling calls after you purchase it—show how options can be traded either independently or in conjunction with shares you already own. This is an important distinction that is often lost on people in the discussion of options, even those who claim to be experts on the subject.

Detractors are fond of saying that options "end up worthless 80% of the time." That sounds awfully damning, as it implies an 80% failure rate. As we illustrated in the examples above, however, options are typically traded well before their expiration date, meaning that traders are closing their positions early and therefore rendering this 80% figure virtually meaningless.

Many day traders who use options rarely let their contracts turn into stock unless they have to. Instead, they "scalp" profits using only the option premiums. Although this term might be pejorative on a street outside Chicago's Soldier Field, it simply refers to the legitimate and daily business of buying and selling options just as investors do with stock, except with much shorter time frames and smaller profits. For these traders, the last thing they want to do is hold options until they expire because their premiums tend to decline with their lifespan, as this so-called time decay eats away at their value until there's almost nothing left. This explains that 80% figure.

But longer-term traders and investors may hold options for much more extended durations, especially if they are waiting for particular events that may affect the stock price. Or they may well want to keep them all the way until expiration, or close to it, if they are holding them as some form of protection.

---

*Purchasing stock risks
losing the entire amount.
Options cost a fraction,
so less is risked.*

YOU'RE IN GOOD HANDS WITH OPTIONS

There is clearly a lot of misinformation out there, and many people think that options and other derivatives are dangerous, high-risk trading vehicles. Billionaire investor Warren Buffett, the famed "Oracle of Omaha," has often been quoted (and misquoted) as having derided derivatives as "financial weapons of mass destruction."

But according to a Bloomberg report on Berkshire Hathaway's 2012 results, "Fourth-quarter earnings rose 49% on gains tied to derivatives wagers by billionaire chairman and chief executive officer Warren Buffett." In his annual letter to shareholders Buffett himself said that "these derivatives have provided a more-than-satisfactory result, especially considering the fact that we were guaranteeing corporate credits—mostly of the high-yield variety—throughout the financial panic and subsequent recession."

It is true that, if left in the wrong hands, options can be dangerous. But in reality, when used properly and prudently, they can actually be safer than many other forms of investment, including stock trading. In fact, options are among the most effective tools available to reduce risk. Although many focus on the earnings power of buying calls, the use of protective puts can be just as important—or more, when things are going south in a hurry.

Just as a call locks in the purchase price of a stock regardless of how far it might rise, a put locks in the sale price no matter how far its underlying shares might fall.

> **Example:** You own 100 shares of Company B, which is trading at $50 (for a total investment of $5,000). The next earnings report is coming up in a few weeks, and you're afraid that the stock could get hammered because of weak demand for its products in the last quarter.

Let's say you can buy a put at the 48 strike for $3. That will cost a total of $300 (as 1 option equals 100 shares), but you will be guaranteed the right to sell the stock for no lower than $48, even if it drops to zero. Granted, you will lose that $300 if the stock stays above the $48 strike price, but that would be far more preferable than having no insurance and losing a whole lot more money if the stock plummets.

But why can't you just program a stop-loss with your stock brokerage that triggers a sell order below a certain level? Good question. You certainly can do that, but there is no guarantee that the order will actually be filled at the price you want. That became painfully clear to many in the "flash crash" of May 6, 2010.

On that day, the S&P 500 saw a massive swing of 102 points, the third-largest move in the index's history. Procter & Gamble, typically one of the most stable blue-chip names on the market, saw its stock price drop by more than a third at the height of the frenzy. Others fell by similar magnitude, and thousands of orders were never filled as exchanges were overloaded with transactions at wildly differing prices driven by gyrations in volatility.

That included huge numbers of stop-loss orders that were never even seen, let alone executed. Remember, even in this age of human-free trading floors, someone or something needs to carry out orders filed online or in person. But when millions of shares are moving in milliseconds, there is no guarantee that a buy or sell order will be made at the level requested in real time.

In the case of the flash crash, let's say you had a stop-loss at $60 when PG was trading around $61. In the blink of an eye, the stock dove from that level to below $40, long before your order could make it through your brokerage and exchange systems. Although those processes function adequately when things are normal, the seconds that they normally take to complete can seem like hours when the Dow Jones Industrial Average is plummeting 600 points in 5 minutes.

Options, however, are cast in stone no matter what is happening in the markets. They are binding contracts that must be honored at given prices and expirations, which is why traders pay premiums for them. And that additional price is peanuts compared to the money that can be saved in a crash.

> **Example:** If you had owned 100 shares of PG at $60, you would have been sitting on a $6,000 investment. To protect those shares, you bought a May 60 put at the price of $.50, for a total cost of $50 (1 put x $.50 x 100 shares). That contract gave you the right to sell PG at $60 a share no matter how far it fell.

If the stock had remained above that $60 strike price, you would have lost the $50 paid for the put. But it didn't—it fell to $39.37 in the flash crash, which means that you theoretically could have lost more than $2,000. So that $50 insurance premium wouldn't look so bad after all, especially when stop-loss orders are essentially being ignored on the way down.

Many professional portfolio managers said the flash crash forever changed their thinking about hedging. One of them is Joe Clark, who was overseeing $180 million in client assets at Indianapolis-based Financial Enhancement Group at the time. "You're better off owning the puts at this point than trying to use stop-loss orders," Clark told optionMONSTER a few days later. He said his firm had been using traditional hedging methods to protect investments for years but, because of what he saw in the crash, "we are exploring options to increase our use."

Jim Paulsen, who was overseeing $375 billion of assets at Wells Capital Management in Minnesota at that time, agreed. "We were verging on having financial markets become dysfunctional, driving the fundamentals as opposed to reflecting the fundamentals." Even though Wells didn't have problems with execution, he said: "If it keeps up in that regard, you would be looking for ways to deal with it."

The unfortunate reality is that it often takes a disaster to understand the true value of insurance. But with fears of the unknown pervading the market today, the use of options for protection is becoming more popular even among committees that run enormous endowments and pension funds. "They're saying, 'It's insufficient for us to count on a diversified portfolio,'" said Jim Gocke, head of institutional research and investigation for the Options Industry Council trade group.

This growing awareness of hedging through options has brought the term "VIX" into the public domain. The VIX is the ticker symbol for the CBOE Volatility Index, which has been dubbed "the fear index" on CNBC and elsewhere because it usually rises when stocks drop, and vice versa. In reality it is far more complex than that, as it measures the implied volatility of S&P 500 options. But for purposes of this discussion we will just note that people tend to view it as a barometer of bearishness in the market. (To show how far the VIX has penetrated the mainstream, a novel titled "The Fear Index" by Robert Harris became a best seller in 2012.)

The VIX is also important in terms of hedging because it has become a major tool for traders. Although the volatility index itself cannot be traded, its options and futures are frequently used to hedge positions in equities. The VIX has been around for about a decade but was not widely known outside professional circles until the market crashed in 2008. It quickly gained notoriety because it had been around the 20 level in September of that year before the mortgage bubble burst, but then spiked to almost 90 when the stock market crashed the next month.

Because of that startlingly inverse correlation, people began looking toward VIX options as a comprehensive hedge for their portfolios. Jamie Tyrrell of Group One Trading says he sees the change every day on the floor of the Chicago Board Options Exchange (CBOE), where his firm is the primary market maker for VIX options. "We're seeing more daily volume, seeing more orders and seeing more bodies. There are a lot of brokers in the pit who don't have enough spots who just stand behind it. It's pretty clear there are a lot more people playing now than in 2007 through 2009."

While individual puts are often purchased to protect particular stocks, as in the case of PG described earlier, traders are increasingly buying VIX calls for broader protection against a crash. If the volatility index shoots up when the market tanks, the thinking goes, why not just buy VIX calls that make money when volatility rises rather than mess around with individual stock puts? And even though broad hedges could be done by buying puts in the S&P 500 and other indexes, the VIX seemed to carry more potential leverage because of its extreme moves.

In the week leading up to the 2010 flash crash, for instance, the VIX soared more than 125% while the S&P 500 fell 12%. "When outliers happen, the VIX goes up so fast. You don't have to spend a lot for protection," said Larry McMillan, the president of McMillan Analysis Group and an author of many best-sellers on options. He's right, of course, but the point is to buy VIX calls when premiums are still reasonable, not after those 125% spikes.

The best analogy is to think of how much we use insurance in other areas. We insure homes, cars, heirlooms, and even our lives, so why wouldn't we insure our investments? And when we do decide to buy that insurance, it's best to do so when times are calm and premiums are low—not when a major storm is heading in our direction.

The same is true for the markets. Whether buying puts in individual stocks or calls in the VIX, prices are sure to accelerate northward as the risk of danger increases. Alan Lancz, president of Toledo, Ohio-based Alan B. Lancz & Associates, sums it up succinctly: "We use options to protect when the VIX is really low because the protection is cheaper when you don't need it."

The key is not to get lulled into complacency, dismissing potential warning signs as just more of the perennial doomsaying of permabears. But that is easier said than done, especially when the markets are going higher. This is where we must pay heed to another breed of the financial jungle, the dreaded "black swan"—a term popularized by the Nassim Taleb book of the same name, which he defines as an event marked by "rarity, extreme impact, and retrospective predictability." It is the last of these three qualities that is the most elusive to grasp, as even modest success can blind us to the possibility of much larger peril.

To insure your portfolio, you are better off owning puts than using stop-loss orders.

TRADER PSYCHOLOGY 101

"Some people think football is a matter of life and death. I assure you, it's much more serious than that." —Bill Shankly

We often talk about the similarities between our experiences in football and trading. The overall keys to success in both worlds are hard work and discipline, but that's just the beginning. In fact, the clichéd sound bites in interviews on ESPN every night can easily be applied to all types of situations in the markets. All it takes is a little imagination to see the parallels:

Defense Wins Championships. Always be aware of how much money you are risking to make money. Smart portfolio management is all about the risk/reward ratio—which means you don't risk $10,000 to make $500.

It's Three and Out. Despite what you may read in the financial press, investing isn't all about high-frequency trading. You don't make more money simply by investing faster. Do your homework and prudently enter and exit your trades.

They Brought Their 'A' Game. Sometimes when a CEO runs a conference call after a great earnings report that beats estimates, he or she will capitalize on the high profile to deliver even more good news, such as positive guidance, a stock buyback, or a special dividend.

Drive for Show and Putt for Dough. Picking a great stock to buy is only half the job; you also must take profits when you get them. Too often we hear of folks who bought a stock just at the right time and rode it higher, only to neglect taking some or all of their stakes off the table. That is usually a recipe for disaster.

Trading Plays on Two Basic Human Instincts: Greed and Fear. It's amazing how quickly we can switch from one to the other, and then back again, minute by minute when watching the markets. But it is often the second of those opposing forces—fear—that ultimately drives success. When considering a trade, many investors ask themselves this question: "How much can I make?" Conversely, Mark Fisher, one of the largest and most successful traders in the world, always says the first question to ask is: "How much can I lose?"

Perhaps this is why we were drawn to trading from our backgrounds in the NFL. Not only were we on the defensive side of the ball, but we also played middle linebacker—a position that required us to be alert to simultaneous threats on the field from all directions. Those instincts have served us well on the trading floor, where we were able to apply our spider senses in a different but equally effective way.

Wall Street is very much like professional sports. A winning trade makes the endorphins pop the same way they do when a stadium fills with cheers. At the same, there are darker similarities between the two professions. On the football field, athletes will hesitate to wear a knee brace for fear that it will encourage adversaries to attack their weakest point. That is precisely what happened to Bear Stearns in March of 2008 when its liquidity problems attracted sharks like blood in the water.

We spotted the unusual option activity in Bear which provided the first clues that a feeding frenzy was about to begin. Little did we know that the scenario would be repeated with Lehman Brothers months later and that it foreshadowed the death of Wall Street as we knew it, but our instincts and experience put us on high alert for disruptions and opportunities.

Like Intel's famed Andy Grove, who penned the famously titled book "Only the Paranoid Survive" and lived by that motto, the best traders are those who anticipate what can go wrong, not just what can go right. This, by the way, should not be mistaken for timidity; quite the opposite, in fact. An old expression on the floors of the stock and option exchanges was "hedging is for wimps." Not surprisingly, the Neanderthals who believed that were not long for the financial world. Those of us who preferred to be rich rather than perceived as more manly have relied heavily on hedging to survive and prosper through the market meltdowns of 1987, 2000, 2008, and briefly in 2010.

Top traders, like the best athletes, are able to balance confidence and skepticism. One must have the confidence to pull the trigger but maintain enough skepticism to stay out of trouble. You may have heard the advice, "Don't fall in love with a stock." Along those lines, we often hear that someone is "married" to a position. In both cases traders may profess their affection out of belief in the company, but more often it comes down to plain old ego: Too many traders obstinately hold onto positions simply because they refuse to admit that they are wrong.

Psychologists say that there's more to this than just stubbornness. There is another old saying on Wall Street, that the markets can stay irrational longer than you can stay solvent. But in his book titled "Predictably Irrational," behavioral economics professor Dan Ariely takes a different approach to this notion, saying that it is people who are irrational even though they think of themselves as rational. This is when good traders apply their skepticism to themselves.

If we know that it is natural for us to think in irrational ways, then we must challenge our previous assumptions. Specifically, where we assume that our reasons for getting into a trade are still valid, we should reexamine it anew and ask ourselves, "Would we enter this position at its current level?" If the answer is no, then we should get out of it, but many people never do this because they don't reexamine their trades in this fashion.

Once we acquire this ability to continually evaluate our actions, we can then turn that lens to the behavior of others as well. This is even more valuable when combined with other forms of research, such as technical analysis. We can better anticipate levels of support or resistance on a stock's chart by analyzing areas where others are likely to enter or exit positions. And people can be "predictably irrational," for example, in targeting a certain levels to sell an underperforming stock because that will "get their money back" regardless of other factors that can help determine its longer-term prospects.

Other studies show that the pain of losing is actually greater than the pleasure of winning because the ideas become part of our self-image. Trading adds another layer of complexity to this concept because it involves our views of money—both practical and emotional—and how it relates to our measure of success.

One of the most interesting research findings in behavioral finance recently is centered on notions of relative wealth. Specifically, studies have focused on the idea that how much we make matters less than how much we make in comparison to those around us. If you make $100,000 when people around you make $60,000, you will be happy. But if you are surrounded by people who make $200,000, you will be unhappy. This may seem like common sense, but it has interesting implications for a number of areas in the investment realm. One of the biggest issues with individual traders, especially new ones, is managing expectations—both in terms of returns and winning percentage. Many new traders expect to be right 70% to 90% of the time. That is simply unrealistic and results in quick disappointment, which in turn leads traders to abandon strategies that are often successful in the long run.

Most research shows that even the best traders are right 40% to 50% of the time at most. Starting with this knowledge will help you set realistic goals and be more patient with your trading ideas and systems. By necessity you have to let your winners run and cut your losers short. But because you expect to be wrong fairly often, it is much easier to admit it and move on, thereby exiting bad positions earlier.

It's not unusual to see late-night infomercials and Internet ads promising that their strategies and systems will turn $10,000 into $3 million in one year, or some other ridiculous claim. It is important to remember that trading is not a get-rich-quick trick. George Soros' Quantum Fund, one of the most successful long-term hedge funds in history, averaged returns of 30% a year in its heyday. Renaissance Technologies founder James Simons, often considered one of the best hedge-fund managers in the business, has averaged 35% a year.

Good traders are like good scientists: They come up with an idea and then set out to prove it false, just like the vetting process for a scientific hypothesis. They don't assume that they are right and work from that assumption. Scientific methodology is based on trying to discredit wrong ideas, not prove them, and traders can take a similar approach by removing certain factors from the equation.

Before opening a position, for instance, a trader should clearly define the thesis, including its potential "edge." But the trader must also determine what conditions would prove the thesis wrong. Often when a CEO makes a guest appearance on "Fast Money," you will hear us ask, "What keeps you up at night?" That same question should be asked of ourselves about specific positions to help anticipate risks and threats. And if you are fortunate enough to see the trade go your way, it's just as important to consider taking at least some money off the table or exiting altogether. That's why you will also frequently hear us say: "Pigs get fat; hogs get slaughtered."

THE CASE FOR OPTIONS

Although we try to apply clinical analysis whenever possible, we're not robots and rarely see things only in black-and-white terms. That is what makes options ideal for trading, as they allow for greater flexibility to express varying degrees of opinion about a stock and where it might go. If an investor just buys and sells stock, he or she is pretty much confined to making a binary bet that the share price will go up or down. Options can express opinions on a wide variety of fronts, including price ranges, time frames, and even a belief that a stock won't move at all.

We've all heard of the death of buy-and-hold stock strategies that have been a hallmark of investing for the last century, talk that has accelerated with each market crash. One of today's more popular terms for successful trading is "nimble," as in describing what it takes to navigate the increasingly turbulent waters of today's markets. This argues in favor of trading vehicles more akin to smaller and faster PT boats than the lumbering battleships of previous generations.

And one of the biggest advantages of options over stocks is "leverage"—the ability to get more bang for your buck by amplifying returns, sometimes exponentially, from relatively small outlays. Options allow you to profit from gains in a stock for far less money without buying the shares outright.

> **Example:** Let's say it's January and Company C is trading at $50 a share, but you think that it will hit $60 after it releases a new product in two months. You can buy 1,000 shares at $50 apiece, spending $50,000 up front. Or, if you want to leverage your position, you could buy $25,000 with your own money and the rest with $25,000 "on margin," which requires you to pay interest to your brokerage.

Using options, you could express the same bullishness by buying 10 March calls for, say, a premium of $2 per share at total cost of $2,000. (Remember, 1 call equals 100 shares, so 10 calls x 100 shares x $2 = $2,000.) That means you have paid $2,000 for the right to buy 1,000 shares at $50 no matter far high the stock might rise.

It seems that your homework is paying off, and the stock is working its way higher with a month to go before that earnings report. In the meantime, the calls that you bought for $2 are now up to $4 as the rest of the market catches up to your bullish thesis.

If the stock does in fact go up to $60, shares that had been bought outright for $50 would make a 20% profit. But the calls you purchased have already made a 100% profit on your $2,000, which is not at all unusual as we frequently see premiums double or triple in this kind of time frame.

In addition to the success and the leverage shown here, this trade is even more impressive for its flexibility at this point. First, you can simply decide to sell the calls for $4,000 and double your money. Or, if you think that the calls will appreciate even more in value, you have another month before they expire. You can also exit the position and "roll" it to contracts at a later expiration and/or a higher strike, perhaps taking some money off the table in the process. And if you get really bullish on the company and want to own the stock, and you can exercise the calls and buy the shares at their original strike price. There are several other possibilities, but these should give you an idea of why traders prefer options for the many alternatives they afford.

Yet perhaps more than anywhere else in option trading, this is where the confidence-versus-skepticism ratio is crucially important. Although leverage can be one of the best advantages of trading options, it is also at the root of practically every major financial collapse in recent memory. Lehman Brothers and some of the other banks at the center of the mortgage crisis were reported to have levered their bets up to 38-to-1 ratios, meaning that they had borrowed $38 for every $1 at stake in many trades. And we know how that ended.

Why would someone take this kind of risk? All too often, the willingness to lever up in increasingly large multiples comes from success breeding a sense of infallibility. Even in the most successful hedge funds, with vast staffs and resources, managers can become so enamored of their investment models that they become blind to the realities of the market.

One of the highest-profile examples of this came from Long Term Capital Management, the hedge fund founded by legendary Salomon Brothers bond trader John Meriwether, who famously stared down Chairman John Gutfreund in a $10 million bet in "liar's poker," according to Michael Lewis' book of the same name. Managers of that fund—whose team included Nobel Prize winners Myron Scholes and Robert Merton—became so smitten with their homegrown investment models that they became blinded to the realities of the market.

Then in 1998 the fund collapsed in such spectacular fashion (or "blew up," in trader terminology) that it required a bailout by other Wall Street firms to avoid a potential domino effect that could take down the market. Yet the creators of LTCM's option-pricing model believed that the type of losses it eventually suffered were "so freakish as to be unlikely to occur even once over the entire life of the universe and even over numerous repetitions of the universe," wrote Roger Lowenstein in "When Genius Failed: The Rise and Fall of Long-Term Capital Management." Amazingly, however, it turns out that the firm's model didn't even factor in the crash of 1987!

There are many lessons here, but three immediately come to mind. First, despite their nomenclature, it's clear that many hedge funds don't hedge very well. Second, leverage is a double-edged sword that can giveth at first but then taketh away far more. Third, confidence can become a liability when not kept in check. And that may be the most important education of all.

Options' biggest advantage is "leverage"—the ability to amplify returns from relatively small outlays.

PROFITING FROM PATIENCE

"Throughout all my years of investing, I've found that the big money was never made in the buying or the selling. The big money was made in the waiting."
—Jesse Livermore

There are many definitions for the poker term "playing on tilt," but it essentially means rushing into a bet because of emotion, often in anger at losing the previous hand. It's not a good idea in poker, and it can be much worse in trading. People tend to bristle at the comparison of trading and gambling, but the parallels are too close to ignore. And it is actually important to understand the similarities so that you can discern the differences.

For example, bad gamblers may make irrational decisions based on little more than a hunch. But the good ones will weigh their decisions based on probability—including the alternative of doing nothing at all. "Mr. Market is there to serve you, not guide you," Warren Buffett once wrote. "If he shows up some day in a particularly foolish mood, you are free to either ignore him or to take advantage of him, but it will be disastrous if you fall under his influence."

This leads to a common trap that many traders fall into: acting simply because they feel the need to do something. Here again is where we can learn a lesson from the best gamblers, in betting big only when the time is right. Charlie Munger, Buffett's longtime partner at Berkshire Hathaway, has this to say about the smartest gamblers: They "bet heavily when the world offers them that opportunity. They bet big when they have the odds. And the rest of the time, they don't."

But unlike at the craps table or the roulette wheel, where players rely mostly on the law of averages, traders have other means to get "an edge." This can include such factors as earnings reports, management changes, new products, currency trends, political events, and even the weather. That's a lot more to chew on than trying to remember how many face cards you've seen when the blackjack dealer is showing a 6 of clubs.

All of these variables play into a key way that we assess a potential trade. Case in point: When the federal government was facing the twin blows of tax hikes and spending cuts in so-called fiscal cliff toward the end of 2012, military contractors had a huge target on their backs. But when Congress and the White House appeared to be heading toward some form of resolution, those defense companies snapped right back. Because of the relatively fixed time frames dictated by the legislative process, option traders were able to buy and sell contracts at particular expiration dates that coincided with Washington deadlines.

This brings also brings us back to the use of options and stocks together. In the above example, you might have owned shares in an aircraft maker as a long-term investment but were worried about the temporary fluctuations from that budgetary standoff. You could have bought puts to protect your position on the way down and then sold calls on the way up if irrational exuberance propelled premiums at strike levels that were way higher than you thought the stock would ever reach.

In the latter case, it is this type of mispricing that is another important way that we can get an advantage with options. We believe that it is a lot easier to identify mispriced options than stocks, partly because of how large institutional investors—such as hedge funds, pension funds, and investment banks—are trading them. optionMONSTER's tracking systems, for example, can spot huge movements by these major players on a tick-by-tick basis. So when we see 10,000 calls purchased at a particular strike and expiration, it is likely that the buyer believes that those options are priced cheaply, or at least reasonably. The opposite can be true with heavy selling.

Although the use of options have grown far faster than equities in the last decade, the volumes of contracts are still much lower in absolute terms. That makes it much easier to spot unusual activity, which our Heat Seeker® and Depth Charge systems show every day. The combination of this kind of microscopic "tell" with fundamental research and technical analysis can provide a unique, holistic view of the landscape for a particular stock or sector. That gives us a better vantage point to see if the herd is going in the right or wrong direction. The best opportunities often come when we think that the market is wrong about something, giving us more potential for outsized gains.

As with everything, however, the devil is in the details. This is why we recommend keeping a trading journal to track your observations and strategies before, during, and after making a move. It's arguably even more important to write down what did NOT work, as well as what did. Why? Because if we don't learn from our mistakes, as we all know, we are doomed to repeat them. This applies not just to individual trades and companies, but to the way we approach the market in general. The hyperspeed of today's financial world means that huge moves are made in nanoseconds, but trading is a marathon. In that vein, one of our primary principles is to know thyself before doing anything else.

> *It's easier to identify mispriced options than stocks because we can follow large investors.*

PART TWO:
A Brief History of Options Trading
(and why you should care)

In this section, "How We Trade Options" looks back at some of the more memorable trading we've seen over the past 25 years, with an eye toward what it means for the future. Our goal is to provide first-person accounts from the floor to recall important lessons for traders, then and now.

Some of what follows was written at the time, and some in retrospect; some was authored by Jon, and some by Pete. To maintain authenticity, whenever sensible we've sought to preserve our original voices.

BEFORE TRADING WAS DIGITAL
HOW WE HELPED OPTIONS EVOLVE

Nowadays it's pretty much assumed that you can trade practically any asset from anywhere in the world. So it might surprise some people to know that there was a time when option trading not only required a physical presence, but in many cases was confined to specific locations around the country.

For example, IBM traded on the CBOE in Chicago, Dell on the Philadelphia Stock Exchange, and Microsoft on the Pacific Stock Exchange in San Francisco. This provincial system created an environment that was not very competitive, and the bid/ask spreads were huge—often 1/4 to 1/2 wide, back in the days when we used fractions. That might sound small until you consider that we now trade in spreads which are often only a penny wide.

So our firm, Mercury Trading, set out to do something about that, starting with one name that was particularly popular at the time. And that work eventually led to widespread changes in the way options were handled on all exchanges.

The focus of our efforts was Micron, one of the hottest option trades back in the mid-'90s. The Pacific Stock Exchange—which we called "P-Coast," as it used to be the Pacific Coast Stock Exchange—had 90% of the order flow in that name, while we had only 5%.

My ultra-competitive nature as a former NFL linebacker just wouldn't stand for that, so I made it my mission to get more of that business. But it soon became clear that our pit alone couldn't put a dent in the San Francisco flow. That's when I got a radical idea: recruit traders from other pits, something that wasn't done in those days.

In just six months we became the most active trading pit at the CBOE. We got up to 20%, then 30%, and sometimes more than 50% of the order flow in Micron contracts. Our pit grew from about 8 or 10 traders to 50 or 60 in a year, and we even had to call in others for help, including my brother Jon from his office upstairs.

We had a system that involved three guys strategically situated in the pit, including Jon and myself, to control the chaotic activity that was spilling over into the aisles. It was our own version of the "triangle offense" that Phil Jackson was using to lead the Bulls to championships just a few miles away on West Madison!

More important, the larger order flow and increased liquidity allowed us to tighten the bid/ask spreads. And that made the options more attractive to trade, which was good for everybody. — **P.N.**

My ultra-competitive nature as a former NFL linebacker forced me to take action.

IN THE EYE OF A DOT-COM STORM

You'd never know it by looking at the sparsely populated trading floors today, but there was a time when a good spot to stand in the pits was worth its weight in gold—literally. This was especially true back in the dot-com era, which was truly a new frontier because fledgling stocks were coming out all the time and no one had an established claim to trade them.

> **America Online was a perfect example:** We had to get to the exchange before 6 a.m. CT to get good spots, which were first-come/first-served, and traders would make a mad dash across the exchange to secure them once the doors opened. Even if you got one, you had to wait another 2-1/2 hours before the market opened without as much as a cup of coffee or a doughnut because no food or drinks are allowed on the floor.

So it wasn't long before traders started paying people just to wait in line and hold spots until trading began. And, like any other free market, the bidding for such services rose with demand. I knew of a case where a guy made more than $50,000 in one year, essentially just to be a spot holder. Not bad for just a few hours of work every morning!

You might think it's nuts for someone to pay this kind of money, but you have to understand how important it was to have that spot. Physical proximity was everything back then: A good spot allowed you to make first contact with brokers, easily reach the book behind you, and get people's attention right away when you wanted to buy or sell.

Then, when the bell rang, the floodgates would burst open. It seemed that companies were being created overnight and going public the next day. And the craziest part of it all was that, all too often, no one could really tell one apart from another.

For a lot of names, it was essentially a binary bet: It was either going to the moon, Netscape-style, or would crash and burn—nothing in between. I remember asking half-jokingly about another new company, "How do we know it's not just three guys in a garage in their underwear and T-shirts, not making any money?"

Because the stocks were so new, they traded in an area called the "green room," named for the color of its walls, which began as a makeshift pit next to the cafeteria to handle options that the CBOE took over from the New York Stock Exchange. Not surprisingly, it soon became the place to be once the dot-com boom began.

There was one quadrant that happened to be where the craziest dot-com action took place, so I assigned a particularly aggressive young trader there. He was trading Akamai when it was over $300 a share.

I went to check on him one time in January 2000, before the crash, and it happened to be the day when AOL and Time Warner announced their merger. It was so crazy, with guys screaming at the top of their lungs and paper flying everywhere. I couldn't resist, so I dove in and started trading myself.

Little did any of us know that the bubble would burst only a few months later. — P.N.

Trading dot-coms was a binary bet, either to the moon or crash and burn.

THE CRASH OF 2008
THE RISE AND FALL OF BEAR STEARNS

When first I came to LaSalle Street in Chicago, Illinois and then to Wall Street in New York, I took it as a badge of honor that I cleared Bear Stearns.

Just one look at the company's letterhead said it all: offices in New York, London, Frankfurt, Shanghai, Tokyo, San Francisco. Bear was truly a global player. Sales trading, research, conferences, market making, investment banking, stock loan, corporate finance, correspondent clearing—you name it. If a firm could make money from a particular business, Bear Stearns was in it.

Bear and its directors made billions of dollars from these businesses. The company was a force to be reckoned with, and that created both admiration and enemies. The problem is that admirers rarely help you as much as the enemies can hurt you.

As I've said many times, Wall Street is very much like professional sports. Though traders rarely get applause (my brother Pete on CNBC's "Fast Money" being a notable exception!), when you've got a winning trade the endorphins pop the same as if prompted by the crowd's cheers. Money simply replaces applause.

Then there are the darker similarities to professional sports. For example, athletes will hesitate to wear a knee brace, for fear that it puts a target on your weakness. Once they know how to hurt you, rivals will concentrate their efforts on attacking you at your weakest point.

This is precisely what happened to Bear Stearns over the past week when competitors learned BSC had liquidity problems. Bear put a target on their weakness and their competitors went for it the same way a shark reacts to the smell of blood in the water. First it's one, then two, then you've got a feeding frenzy.

Most of you know how brokerage firms like Bear Stearns make money. The commission business is just one of several revenue streams available to them.

The others include stock loan, the lending of securities to market makers and hedge funds that have shorted stocks, seeking to repurchase them at lower prices. The shorts must secure a lender that has the shares on its books, especially for hard-to-borrow issues. This is an incredibly lucrative business.

Another is mergers and acquisition, where the broker takes 7% or more as a fee to put the buyer and seller together, and may or may not provide financing as well, again at a price. Still another is fixed income trading, where the broker profits from the buying and selling of government, corporate, and municipal bonds.

But some of the most profitable and safest business for any broker is taking the spread on the differential between excess money on deposit and lending that money to finance margin loans. Especially in an environment like this one, where an activist Federal Reserve has crushed short-term rates to 3%, the difference between the interest paid on free cash and that charged to support margin loans can widen to 5 or more points.

In a perfect world, Bear Stearns might have $5 billion in free cash that it is paying 3 to 4% on and charging 6 to 8% on the other side for the margin loans. The math for 5 points on $5 billion is $250 million, and all you've really done is balance your book, matching excess against demand. But when that excess cash decided to leave, Bear was left holding the bag and it was a bag they couldn't lift.

When I speak of placing a target on your weakness, I am saying that chief executive Alan Schwartz's comments demonstrably failed to calm the markets. Instead, they confirmed the company was in deep trouble. The blood was in the water, and Bear's competitors wasted no time in letting everyone know that their money was not safe at BSC.

As cash was pulled, Bear struggled to meet the demand and had to go begging, hat in hand, nay even on their hands and knees. Not a pretty sight and that accelerated the calls for cash as rumors of the liquidity crisis spread faster than the stories of former CEO Jimmy Cane's drug abuse.

As Mr. Schwartz said last Friday in that now-infamous conference call with investors: "People wanted to get cash out, and at the pace we were going, the continued liquidity demands would outstrip our liquidity resources." In those desperate days, for the first time Mr. Schwartz was talking straight. Now 14,000 employees and millions of investors wish that the leadership at Bear hadn't been fiddling while the 85-year old firm burned. — J.N.

THE RUN ON LEHMAN AND WHAT COMES NEXT

The last few weeks have been full of rumors of this bank or that brokerage going out of business. Trading floors and desks were buzzing about whether Bear Stearns, Lehman, or even Goldman Sachs might have to seek governmental bailout if not file for bankruptcy. While some of the chatter was relatively easy to dismiss, some, sadly, was all too believable.

I remember being on a conference call this past fall listening to the leaders of Bear Stearns trying to shore up confidence in their battered company. As I said then, the plausibility of how things could possibly be positive at Bear escaped me. Here was the chairman, Jimmy Cayne, out playing golf while the firm bled. The Wall Street Journal reported that at least one of Mr. Cayne's bridge competitors had joined the CEO for a little recreational drug use, and Mr. Cayne's denial was taken about as seriously as a tabloid headline proclaiming an alien in disguise running for president.

Therefore it came as no surprise that Bear was the first firm to fall, but what was surprising was just how fast it fell. The implosion of Enron and WorldCom came after months of headlines, congressional hearings, and price contraction. Bear Stearns went from $70 to $2 in a week! The value of Mr. Cayne's 5.6-million share stake in BSC deteriorated from $392 million to just $11.2 million over that tumultuous time. So if he needed drugs to escape the market volatility over the summer and fall, one can only imagine what diversion he deemed necessary given his sudden change of fortune.

Set Up To Fall Down

In the Bear Stearns situation our computers picked up strong, unusual buying of puts, which didn't surprise us given the impossibly confusing alphabet soup of derivatives that Bear was responsible for either packaging, trading, or holding. What did surprise us was the heavy buying of way, way out-the-money puts. Under normal circumstances smart money traders don't make dumb bets: They don't buy puts that give them the right to sell at $25 for a stock that is trading for $65, because if they thought it could drop to $25, why not participate on the $40 slide from $65 to $25?

The fact that they were so aggressively buying these puts, which we termed "bankruptcy puts," meant they were betting that the broker would be dealt a death sentence and be forced into liquidation. It turned out they were wrong about bankruptcy, but only because the Fed and JP Morgan stepped in. The put buyers were dumb like a fox and cashed in huge, making hundreds of millions of dollars out of single-digit millions in downside bets.

Lehman Next?

Clearly there was very active speculation that Lehman will follow Bear Stearns down the rat hole. I say this because the put buying accelerated dramatically over the final two days of last week. At first our computers were reading puts being purchased that were just out, or at-the-money, meaning the activity was in the 40 puts with LEH trading above that level. But on Thursday the 27th, the buying spread from those typical smart money bets to the bankruptcy puts, as buying of the 25 and 20 put contracts surged from mid-session into the close.

While the activity was neither as big nor as aggressive as the feeding frenzy in Bear, it's important to note that as these puts exploded in price on Thursday, the volatility, or expected risk, of Lehman sky rocketed. For example, even as the financial stocks were rocked by the Bear Stearns implosion over the past two weeks, Lehman volatility danced between 80 and 125. But on March 27, volatility for those out-the-money puts in LEH vaulted to 175!

The volumes of puts traded accelerated through Thursday, but died down substantially Friday. The week had started with some 40,000 puts trading on Monday, followed by 70,000 puts on Tuesday, and another 80,000 puts on Wednesday. That made Thursday's 248,000 puts something to behold! But then the action fell dramatically, as a brokerage upgrade and news of an SEC investigation slowed Lehman's fall on Friday.

I don't believe in fortune tellers, but whenever I see one depicted on TV or in the movies they seem to face a dilemma in "seeing" something negative in the client's future. Much as I don't buy their shtick, I can emphasize as we at optionMONSTER faithfully interpret the data our algorithms and computers find. We are not robots, and make effective use of discretion, but if the "fast money" says buy, generally we buy. When it says that a stock looks like it's going to die, I swallow harder, because I know our call can help accelerate the negative reaction to market events.

The good news for LEH, its employees, and its brokers is that the feeding frenzy on Friday the 28th failed to show up. An upgrade from Citigroup certainly helped, as did the SEC's making know its looking into the question of whether some traders were attempting to create a panic or run on LEH similar to the one in Bear Stearns. Our data tends to support that theory, for as I said, the bulk of the buying centered on the at- or just out-the-money puts in LEH, not those bankruptcy puts.

Only time will tell if the investigation finds some dastardly dudes or dudettes were indeed seeking to manipulate Lehman, but one thing is sure: whether they're buying calls or puts, they can't hide from the Heat Seeker® or Depth Charge®. — **J.N.**

Heavy buying of way, way out-the-money puts was a telltale sign.

THE WORST TRADE IN HISTORY

There are some lists you want to see your name on, and others you'd rather not have anything to do with. It would be nice make the Forbes 400, for instance, but not the obituaries.

When it comes to listing the worst trades of all time, many of you might name Atlanta trading Brett Favre to the Green Bay Packers, or maybe Lou Brock for Ernie Broglio, or the Phillies trading Sandberg and Bowa for Ivan DeJesus.

Yet as bad as those were, they are dwarfed by the worst trade in history, which I am about to reveal.

To paraphrase my friend Mark Fisher, founder of MBF Clearing and one of the biggest energy trader/brokers in the world, the federal government let the trade of the century slip through its fingers at the depths of the financial crisis. Worst of all, the Oracle of Omaha had already drawn the perfect blueprint, in steps so easy that even a Treasury secretary could follow! Doesn't that make the government the worst trading entity of all time?

For those with short memories, like our officials in Washington, I offer the following. Long before he bought Burlington Northern this week, Warren Buffett agreed to invest $5 billion in Goldman Sachs through a purchase of perpetual preferred stock (take note of the "perpetual" reference) on September 23, 2008. The shrewd chairman and CEO of Berkshire Hathaway also got warrants to buy up to $5 billion of Goldman common shares at $115 each, some 8% below where the stock was trading at the time.

In a single bold stroke, when Goldman and the global markets needed it most, Buffett put his money and reputation on the line. He stood to own roughly 10% of the bank, and his convertible shares also pay a fat 10% dividend. Just weeks later John Mack, CEO of Morgan Stanley, completed a long-awaited deal to sell a fifth of his own Wall Street pillar to a big Japanese bank for $9 billion.

Yet even with these trades serving as very public models, what did then-Treasury Secretary Hank Paulson ask for? When he extended billions of government dollars to Goldman Sachs, Morgan Stanley, JP Morgan, Bank of America, and scores of others wounded financial leaders, did he demand Buffett's tough terms?

No. When these Wall Street giants had their backs to the wall, Paulson gives them our taxpayer dollars—*BILLIONS of 'em—for practically nothing!*

Spin forward to October 21st of this year, and now Geithner (former New York Fed president) is telling us what a great investment we made in Goldman. His office touts the 23% return we made on our $5 billion in taxpayer money. Yes, I am glad we made 23%, but before we break our arms patting ourselves on the back, let's consider what we might have gotten under terms similar to those negotiated by Buffett.

In mid-October 2008, Goldman Sachs and Morgan Stanley got $10 billion from the Treasury; Bank of America, Citigroup, JP Morgan, and Wells Fargo got $25 billion. If we, the taxpayers of the United States, had gotten terms similar to Buffett's, here is what investments in just Goldman Sachs and Morgan Stanley would be worth, according to my calculations: Goldman was trading at $115, so a $5 billion stake bought us 43 million shares. With shares running to $180, that $5 billion stake would be worth $7.8 billion, a gain of $2.8 billion. But wait, it gets better—or worse, depending on your view.

Given that additional kicker of warrants on another $5 billion, 8% under the market, we'd also own share equivalent (warrants) of 43 million shares at $105. So we'd have made another $3.2 billion. Thus, the total take before dividends would be $6 billion on a $5 billion investment. Last time I checked, that's 120% on our money, versus the 23% that Hank got us.

I didn't go to Dartmouth as Secretary Paulson did, but I think Buffett got a better deal! Morgan Stanley was at $17, so a $5 billion stake bought us 294 million shares. With the stock running to $34, that $5 billion stake would be worth nearly $10 billion, for a profit of $4.9 billion.

The total take before dividends would be $10.3 billion on $5 billion investment. That's another 206%, versus 20%. Are you kidding me? Hey, if you're not outraged, you're not paying attention! — **J.N.**

LAWS OF THE JUNGLE RULED IN 2008

While listening to the audio version of "Too Big To Fail" in Mexico during the last holiday weekend, the book's shocking revelations came in stark contrast to the soothing sounds of the surf on Puerto Vallarta's beaches.

I had read the tome two months ago, but upon hearing it again I constantly found myself walking away and shaking my head. If you haven't read or heard it yet, I guarantee that you will be enlightened by this book, penned by my friend Andrew Ross Sorkin.

To those of us who have participated in deals done on Wall Street, the timeline of the debacle reinforces how much insider information was available and how compelling—and enriching—it would have been to have possessed that intelligence.

On the second week of September 2008, then-Treasury Secretary Henry Paulson had just finished privatizing Freddie Mac and Fannie Mae and was facing the pending failures of Lehman Brothers, Merrill Lynch, and American International Group. The teams of bankers and lawyers who had descended on the New York Federal Reserve were under the gun to get deals done. But as dire as the situation was at the time, the most damning assessments had been made months earlier.

I was shocked to learn how many bankers at Morgan Stanley and JP Morgan already were gravely aware how bad things were at AIG and Lehman. The information held by these 80 people could have been the equivalent of alchemy, turning seawater into gold. Imagine that you were AIG's banker (JP Morgan) and knew that they didn't have 5 cents on the dollar to cover their obligations and were facing ratings downgrades that would require additional capital of up to $20 billion?

Requesting a sum that large from a firm that was already facing liquidity issues would be like asking for more hours in the day—which, by the way, AIG desperately needed to avoid shutting down. The information these people possessed may well have been the reason we had seen so much put activity in AIG and LEH at that time.

As Gordon Gecko said in Oliver Stone's "Wall Street," information is capital. I will liken what I found, reading or listening through the lines, to the survivors in another movie drama, "Alive"—the story of a rugby team whose plane crashed in the Andes. In that film the survivors stayed alive by eating their deceased comrades.

In Wall Street's equivalent of that story in late 2008, many traders likely survived because they shorted shares of AIG, FNM, FRE, and LEH. In effect, the traders were eating (shorting) the corpses of those mighty institutions to generate some of the capital needed to withstand the full force of the storm.

To be fair, I don't think the traders and bankers enjoyed the taste of this shorting any more than the rugby players enjoyed the flavor of their dead comrades. But as we always say in this business, it's kill or be killed. — **J.N.**

I was shocked to learn how many bankers were aware how bad things were at AIG and Lehman.

CASE STUDIES IN TRADING
YOU NEVER KNOW WHAT WILL GET HOT

One thing I always found curious is why certain names become a magnet for option activity.

Back in the '90s, we fought hard to become the main trading pit that would handle the paper in Sony. Remember, this was long before Steve Jobs returned to Apple, and the iPod didn't even exist—Sony was the king of consumer electronics back then, when the Walkman reigned supreme.

So when we finally did get the right to be the "specialist" in SNE, making us the main conduit for its option flow on the CBOE floor, we thought it was a huge win. But to our surprise, it turned out to be a huge dud. Days would go by without a single quote from a broker.

But you know what name was crazy busy in those days? Snapple. Yes, the same company famous for bottled tea and juices touted by "The Snapple Lady" who answered letters from fans on endless TV commercials back in the day.

Long before it was sold multiple times and finally ended up in the hands of Dr. Pepper, Snapple was the busiest name in our pit in Chicago. It was a crazy stock that traded an enormous number of options on multiple exchanges.

Everyone aggressively traded the name because they wanted big volume for more liquidity, allowed them to create more opportunities and make deep markets. Believe it or not, in those days it was the closest thing to what an Apple or a Facebook is today as far as options are concerned.

One reason that Snapple options were so popular was because it was hard to borrow shares to short the stock. That mean traders bought puts instead when making a bearish bet. And the volatility of the stock made for more volatility in the options, which makes for good trading opportunities.

The truth, though, is that there's no exact reason that any name becomes a huge trading vehicle—it just happens. And it doesn't always mean that it's a good thing for the share price either. — **P.N.**

KEEP YOUR TRADING PERSPECTIVE

With the backdrop of 2008's market collapse, no wonder investors are nervous.

Last September the Dow Jones Industrials were above 11,500 (see chart), and even after a furious rally from the March lows the index is still just over 9,500. As I often say, the situation we're in changes based on which vantage point you choose.

Take volatility as another example. Last September the VIX had readings around 22 as we hit Labor Day, and today we are back near those lows, as the CBOE's risk metric trades 23%. Again, a VIX reading of 23 would seem high against the pre-Bear Stearns debacle of March 2008 and euphorically overconfident when compared with the November readings that topped 90. It's all about perspective, my friends.

The same is true of trading. Pete, Guy Adami, and I laughed out loud when a guest on a nationally televised show on options recently argued that the other's strategy of a covered write in Google was too risky, but then went on to describe a naked put sale as the smarter play. I will explain why that perspective is completely wrong and why the two strategies do in fact carry the exact same risk.

Covered Writes

The covered write is achieved by the purchase (or previous ownership) of shares of a security and the sale of call options against the shares. As an example, let's look at a covered write in IBM. With shares trading for $116 we could purchase 1,000 shares of IBM and sell 10 of the October 115 calls against that share ownership.

Now let's look at the risk/reward of that position: The October 115 call we sold brought in a credit of $5 to our account. With shares purchased for $116 that means our downside break-even at expiration is $111 ($116 - $5 = $111). If shares are $115 or higher as October expiry hits, our shares would be called away at $115, which would mean we have a net profit of $4 ($116 - $5 = $111, called away at $115 = $4).

Naked Put Sale

The naked put sale doesn't require us to disrobe. It is just the sale of a put, which would obligate us to buy shares at that strike price, at the put owner's discretion. Using our IBM example, the naked sale of the October 115 put would generate $4.

If we wanted to take the same risk as the covered write, we would sell 10 of the October 115 puts for $4. Again, let's look at the risk/reward: The October 115 puts we sold brought in a credit of $4 to our account. That means our downside break-even at expiration is $111 ($115 - $4 = $111). If shares are $115 or higher as October expiry hits, we would keep the entire $4 premium we received for the put sale.

Perspective

In both cases, if IBM breaks through $115 we own shares at $111. We have no protection from that level down, just naked long stock. If IBM is higher than $115 we earn the same $4 from the covered write or naked put sale. Now there are considerations that go beyond this single event, such as holding IBM for long-term capital gains or the better leverage in the naked put sale, but the return and the risk of either is precisely the same and would always be so unless the stock was hard to borrow. But that's for another discussion! — **J.N.**

One guy said a covered call was too risky and described a naked put sale as smarter!

CAUTIONARY TALE IN A HIGH FLIER

People often think of dot-coms when they talk about the craziest stock trades, but there was another boom around the same time that also involved the Silicon Valley area. That was in biotechnology, and it's where I got my first true taste of how a feeding frenzy can make a stock get out of control in a hurry.

An interesting change was taking place in the pharmaceutical world in the 1990s. The entire testing and regulatory process seemed to slow down throughout the industry because of nervousness over efficacy and litigation, so a company really stood out when it seemed be making real progress.

One of those names was a small firm called Geron, based in Menlo Park, California. On one particularly sleepy day, I noticed that the option paper was starting to pick up in this little biotech stock in the trading pit next to me, so I offered to help out. The action kept getting busier throughout the session, when shares were trading around $10 or $12.

The next day, all hell broke loose. Trading in Geron was halted because of news, and that news was incredible: The word on the floor was that the company had found a cure for cancer. Before the market opened, the bid was indicated at $50, then $60, then $70, $80, and past $90.

The move was so huge that it even helped make one trader a partner in his firm, as he was fortunate enough to have owned hundreds of upside calls purchased for just 10 cents apiece weeks or months earlier. Those contracts were bought at levels well above the stock price at the time, so many people might have thought that they would end up worthless. But after Geron skyrocketed that day, the exact opposite turned out to be true!

The pit, which normally had just 3 or 4 traders, instantly swelled to 30 or 40 as they jammed in trying to make markets as fast as they could. When I was finally able to break away, I called my father to ask him what he thought of all this, figuring that he might have a professional opinion as an experienced physician.

"Dad, I'm trading this biotech that's gone through the roof. They apparently found a cure for cancer," I said. His response was as unforgettable as it was brief: "No they didn't."

Although he had no details, his instincts were right. As the story unfolded, it turned out that Geron's accomplishments were far more modest than the rumors that propelled the stock to stratospheric levels—and, predictably, shares came tumbling back to earth. Today Geron's stock price is just over $1.

Trading drug companies, especially smaller ones, is sometimes compared to gambling at casinos because it can be an all-or-nothing wager. If its drug is approved, the stock soars; if it is rejected by regulators or proves ineffective, the stock gets hammered.

It was an important education that stuck with me, as it foreshadowed what was to come in the Internet boom and bust. Whenever a new dot-com stock would take off, I would think of it as one of those biotech names: The story was inevitably based on potential more than reality, just like a drug company's "pipeline."

The lesson? That I should always be fully hedged. — **P.N.**

A biotech that reportedly found a cure for cancer went through the roof. The next day ...

HOW MARK CUBAN SAVED HIS FORTUNE

My friend Mark Cuban is known for many things, but not many people are familiar with his acumen in the markets. In fact, perhaps his best trade was one that saved him from losing his fortune.

Long before he became owner of the Dallas Mavericks, Cuban used a collar trade to lock in profits from his $5 billion-plus sale of Broadcast.com to Yahoo at the height of the dot-com bubble. The trade gave Cuban exposure to some upside but limited the downside in a position where he could not sell the stock because of his lock-up period.

This is obviously an extreme example, but it underscores for all of us the value of collar trades in situations where you must own the underlying. They can be designed in a variety of ways to protect positions and/or profits.

Of course, one of the great things about being a retail trader is that you usually don't have to hold onto such positions. And a bull call vertical spread has essentially the same profit/loss profile as a collar without the necessity of owning the stock. The margin requirements are also significantly lower on a call spread than on a collar.

Still, there are other lessons to be learned about the Cuban trade, including the concept of the zero-sum game. This is an idea that trips up a lot of new players in the option market.

If we flip a coin and I get $1 on heads and you get $1 on tails, that is a zero-sum game. But people use options in different ways and for different reasons, so it is far more complex than that.

For instance, when we write about an institution buying or selling a seemingly unusual call or put position, we often get asked about it. (Usually it is the odd out-of-the-money puts that draw the most questions, but calls make for a better example here.)

A few months back we could have bought a SPY March 128 call for $4 with the SPY trading at $126. On March 1, it was worth $10 with the SPY up at $137 or so. So the call buyer profited and the call seller lost—right? Well, not necessarily.

Certainly the outright buyers profited if they had held the calls. They made $6 on a $9 stock move, but it was a 150% option profit. Even as time decay accelerated, the calls went further into the money and produced profits.

But if sellers simply did the trade as a covered call, they profited too. They would have made $2 on the stock move up to $128 and the credit of $4 from selling the call, also for a profit of $6.

The call seller could also have been delta-hedged, which is what market makers do. When you buy a call, the other side of the trade is almost certainly a market maker who immediately hedges the sale with stock. Such hedged positions are essentially selling the implied volatility of the stock and collecting the actual volatility—making profit on the ultimate difference between the two.

The implied volatility of the SPY options at the end of 2011 was around 22%, while the actual volatility last week was less than 8%. So the dealer who sold the call and delta-hedged it also made a very nice profit.

Just because one person turns a profit on options, it doesn't necessarily mean that money was lost on the other side of the trade. Of course, being realistic, it is entirely possible that both sides lose on the play as well.

That's why it's so misleading to call this a simple zero-sum game. — **J.N.**

Mark Cuban's best trade was the one that saved him from losing his fortune.

MANAGING RISK IN BIDDING WARS

We had three recent examples of the greater fool theory on Wall Street: Hewlett-Packard fighting Dell for 3Par, BHP Billiton pursuing Potash, and GlaxoSmithKline targeting Genzyme. In each case it was, or is, believed that someone might come along and pay more than the already-exorbitant bid for each company.

Pete, Guy, and I have played this game for a collective 60 years, and as often as we tell people to take the money and run, someone is out there saying, "Let's see if we can get more." I say those folks are violating the "hog principle" (i.e., pigs get fat, hogs get slaughtered); but we nonetheless see folks who follow that path getting cleaned out on a regular basis.

Unfortunately, too many are otherwise smart option players who have forgotten the basic tenets of trading options — leverage and time decay.

Let's compare the stock investor to the option investor in any takeover situation. The stock investor makes money dollar for dollar as shares pop on the takeover bid. Thus, as POT runs from $110 to $130 on the BHP bid, the stock investor makes $20.

In making $20 on $110 investment, he or she makes 18%. Now this investor may choose to close the position or hold on for more, but the passage of time does not affect it.

Now let's look at the option investor. Say, for instance, that he followed some unusual activity and bought out-the-money $125 or $130 calls on POT ahead of the BHP bid. On the $20 move in underlying shares, the option position probably increased by 100% to 200%; but now the trader/investor must decide pretty quickly whether he should exit completely or sell another strike above that which is owned.

If the trader fails to take prompt action on such a move, the volatility is likely to bleed out rather quickly, and then there's that pesky time decay. In other words, the holder of the option really needs that white knight to step up quickly, as the clock is ticking and the option decay accelerating.

This is why we emphasize taking profits quickly on option trades, at least 50% on any double in naked calls or spreads. We then set a stop. (If you're trading through tradeMONSTER you can have the platform set the exit at the next 50%.) As a rule of thumb, I close the remaining 50% if the option pulls back to under 10% of where I sold the first tranche.

> **Example:** I buy a call (or spread) for $1.25 and, as the stock moves in my direction, the option or spread expands to $2.50—a 100% profit. At that point I sell half my holdings. With the other 50%, I hold on for more.

If the rally (calls) or selloff (puts) fails, then I'd automatically exit the remaining 50% at $2.25. If you manage your risk the same way—don't forget to cut your losses at 50%—I think you'll be a successful trader for years to come. Leave the greater fool trades to the newbies. — **J.N.**

*Time decay
is why we emphasize
taking profits quickly.*

OPTIONS SAVED MY GOOGLE TRADE

Traders took profits early today in Google, and it was the right move.

This is a great stock, and it had been running like a champ ahead of today's earnings release. I was riding that rally with call spreads, an option strategy that lets you really leverage a pop.

But this morning, the options paper showed traders jumping off the bandwagon. Our data systems at optionMONSTER detected heavy selling in the October 800 calls early in the session, which means that traders didn't see much chance of the stock ending the week above that level.

That activity prompted me to exit my longs, and it wound up being a good move before the company's quarterly results were published prematurely and GOOG tanked!

The puts then caught fire, and premiums shot up as investors scrambled for protection. The October 700s, which started the day more than $50 of out the money, were quickly in play and at one point traded for more than $60.

Overall it's been a pretty crazy day for GOOG, which is now halted down 9.03% at $687.30. Even before they stopped the trading, more than 160,000 option contracts had changed hands in the name. That's triple the daily average, and makes it the fifth busiest stock on our systems today. — **J.N.**

THE FLASH CRASH
THEORIES BEHIND THE FLASH CRASH

It's been a month since the May 6 "flash crash," and we still have no official reason for what happened. But here are three possible, some might even say plausible, scenarios.

A Very Possible Explanation - A firm, presumably a hedge fund, executed the trade that was the catalyst for the crash. The only reasonable reason that a fund would do such a thing was that they thought they could manipulate the market. (Remember that Goldman Sachs said last spring that the high-frequency algorithms stolen from them could be "used to manipulate the markets in a bad way.") And prior to that manipulation the firm purchased a significant amount of put options.

Perhaps the Most Likely Scenario - A firm that clears hedge funds (we'll call it Firm A), also known as a prime broker, has a fund that was bleeding. That becomes the prime broker's problem when the firm in question has nearly depleted its capital. At such time the broker freezes the hedge fund's accounts and takes measures to limit its exposure. After analyzing the firm's positions, the broker decides how many futures it must sell.

Just before executing the futures hedge, an unscrupulous member of the team executing the trade tells a friend at a rival prime broker or hedge fund (Firm B) that they are about to hit the market with $300 million in futures. The message could be something as innocuous as, "Can't join you for lunch today, got a big meeting at 3."

The person on the receiving end of the email knows they just have moments to hit the market with $300 million sale (also known as program trade), executing a portfolio of stocks that make up the bulk of the S&P futures that are about to be sold. The problem is that, instead of selling $300 million, an extra digit—not a "B" as in billions versus "M" as in millions—hits far more stock that is bid for in that millisecond.

Then as the futures trade from Firm A hits, the algos do what they are programmed to: shut down. The pressure is too great and as each bid falls, every subsequent bid also falls, creating the proverbial snowball that gets bigger as it gains speed downhill.

Probably the Least Plausible Reason - A firm that has not properly set fail-safe systems in its algo trading programs picks up a bad price for a millisecond and generates a program trade, selling million of shares in the blink of an eye. Other than the obvious issue that the trade was triggered by bad data, the program is executed as other large trades come in and basically freezes as it was built to do when an obvious error occurs.

There would be a freakishly small chance that all these events could occur at the same time. I always say there are no coincidences on Wall Street, and this would fall squarely in the coincidence category.

What happened on May 6th remains a very severe problem on so many levels. The regulators are clearly overmatched in intelligence, resources, and political clout. Absent some dramatic changes that curb the fractionalization of our financial markets, letting firms skirt the rules and affirmative obligations that market makers have on the CME, CBOE, NYSE, and NASDAQ, I think the results the next time could be disastrous. — **J.N.**

*There are
no coincidences
on Wall Street.*

RUMORS OF HEDGE FUND LIQUIDATION

The rumors have been out there all week, about a hedge fund or funds being liquidated, and that certainly could be true. Today's move, particularly in the last hour, makes it feel as though that could indeed be happening.

Someone pulled the trigger on closing a big player yesterday two hours into the bell, and the market then settled down in the final hour. Today they've matched that pattern exactly, but I doubt we will see much calming by the close.

If you have dry powder this is when you deploy, but the smart money may not want to do that into the weekend. It is a perfect storm for the bears, of which I was one!

We show 2.6 to 1 puts trading in the S&P 500 Exchange-Traded Fund (SPY). The May options in the SPY show more than 1.4 million puts trading from a total of 2.2 million puts as of this writing.

On the selloff the VIX followed a scary but predictable pattern: Panic lifts volatility, which is usually met with selling, retracing the VIX to half of its recent gain. This played out, as the volatility index shot to 27.23 yesterday, then pulled back to $23.50. But then that predictable second wave of panic hit, and the volatility popped to new highs today, now nearing 35.

The VIX was coming from a multi-month low in the mid-15s only three weeks ago, indicating that there was little fear and the options were pricing in confidence, or some might say overconfidence.

The options in the farther-out months have expanded like crazy. Here is what the June 2011 straddle at the 1150 strike was and where it is now: Ten days ago the June 2011 1150 straddle priced at $158. Today it is $233—a move of $75, or 47%.

But hang on, that is pricing the straddle at a 25 volatility. If we were to price in 30—the front-month VIX contract has already topped 32—then the straddle would price at $280, a 77% increase! — **J.N.**

MARKET MANIPULATION
WHO KNEW WHAT ABOUT DELL AND PEROT?

We've all dreamed about buying an option for $.55 and having it run to $10. I must confess, it's a reoccurring dream of mine and, in full disclosure, I happily add that I have experienced this feeling on several occasions thanks to our Heat Seeker® and Depth Charge algorithms.

That's not just hyperbole folks—just search for "Najarian" or "optionMONSTER" on the Web and you will see dozens of stories ranging from Hilton's takeover to the collapse of Bear Stearns and Lehman Brothers. Yes, this stuff really does work, which is why Guy, Pete, and I spend so much time staring at these computer screens when nearly everyone else that has such high-speed access spends their time watching singing cats or dancing dogs on YouTube!

The algorithms I cited are the essence of what optionMONSTER is all about. And like most computer systems, it does things that human eyes and brains used to do, but without getting distracted those warbling pets.

In recent trading, we had what I believe is a textbook example of someone knowing something ahead of everyone else—and that something was the $3.9 billion takeover of Perot Systems by Dell announced Monday, Sept. 21.

Dell is chasing IBM and Hewlett-Packard into the services space and, with the acquisition of Perot, the PC maker gets 23,000 worldwide employees in that part of the industry. Which means it then go head to head its rivals on large corporate systems, running services for data centers, project planning, databases, and software management.

Dell CTO Paul Prince says the pending acquisition reflects Dell's goal to strengthen its service operations on the way to becoming a full-scale enterprise technology company. The reason for the acquisition was clear, as IBM has set the standard for merging computing hardware and services, with the latter bringing in nearly 50% of Big Blue's revenue in the last quarter.

Now to that unusually heavy option volume I mentioned earlier: The average daily call volume in PER has been just 33 contracts per day. A grand total of 701 contracts traded in the entire month of August.

But the week before the Dell acquisition was announced was hardly an ordinary one for PER options. It began with 967 calls changing hands on Monday, September 14th. That was followed by 1,351 calls traded on Tuesday and 2,333 on Wednesday, September 15th-16th. Thursday saw 1,089 calls turn over, and on Friday—the last trading session before the 65% pop on the DELL takeover bid—PER traded 2,539 calls.

In other words, that one week represented multi-month volume for PER.

The options that were trading for $.35 to $.55 that Monday through Friday went as high as $10 on the day the deal was announced. How did those trades fare? Imagine a 50 lot of the October 20 calls purchased for $.55, or an investment of $2,750, going to $50,000 in just one day.

When you multiply that by the thousands of contracts that traded last week, you see the temptation for someone with knowledge of a deal to take advantage of it. But when they do, the fingerprints they leave may eventually end up on an arrest blotter! (Editor's note: After this column was published, the Securities and Exchange Commission charged an employee of Perot Systems with insider trading.)

So why didn't we report this activity until after the fact? PER is what we call a "roach motel," a stock that trades only on one exchange (PHLX). We normally avoid single-list equities, as you pay up to enter and pay down to exit—making trades that don't work out far more expensive.

Sure, with 20/20 hindsight we should have been on this one. But if we were, and the deal did not materialize, we would have been stuck trying to wriggle out of that sticky position. — **J.N.**

WHAT TO DO ABOUT HIGH FREQUENCY TRADING

As I said yesterday, there was very suspicious quoting/trading on U.S. exchanges yesterday. Any of us with the ability to "see" the full market picture were rightly thinking we were on the precipice of another flash crash yesterday morning, as the packets of information, bids, offers, orders, cancellations, etc., were topping out in the danger zone.

When this happens all too frequently it is because some nasty high-frequency trader (HFT) with nefarious intent is trying to create latency so that they can pick pockets even faster than they normally do.

I reached out to Sal Arnuk and Joe Saluzzi of Themis Trading as well as some folks that prefer to remain anonymous and asked them if they were seeing similar patterns in data packets and universally the answer was yes!

Eric Hunsader of Nanex answered with the following, which I confirmed with him prior to publishing:

"There was a significant lack of liquidity (on August 3rd). At 10:00 am ET, right before news, depth plummeted to 1K for all 10 levels on bid and ask side (of eMini)! Normally it's 15-20K for all 10 bids and same amount for all 10 asks. Meaning 1000 contracts would have moved the eMini 10 levels or 2.50 points. Normally you only see an entry when there is news or someone is being extra naughty."

Thank you Eric, my sentiments exactly.

I am all for technology and I'm not saying that faster dissemination of information is a bad thing, when in fact I think it is a good thing. However, when high-speed communication is only available to the few and they abuse the power to electronically pick the pockets of investors it is wrong and should be stopped.

As a couple solutions, rather than just complaints, are needed, I offer:

> HFT traders that have no affirmative obligations in the marketplace, but have pushed out those that did have obligations to continuously submit bids and offers. I would make it requisite that HFT players take on such obligations.
>
> Deny dark pools the ability to incent "liquidity providers" that routinely provide a "peak" at orders prior to entry into the dark pool. This "peak" gives the HFT crowd the ability to race ahead of the orders, forcing the buyer to pay more, or the seller to sell lower.
>
> Make the price point for trading universal for all participants. Presently, HFT players can trade in 1/1000th of a penny increments while Joe and Jane investor have minimum tick in securities trading of a penny. This allows HFT to step ahead of orders for one cent per 1,000 shares and is patently unfair and decimates market integrity and ecology.

My hope is someone at the SEC will indeed assess the situation and do the right thing. We've still got the greatest capital markets in the world, even with all these flaws, but if we let an extreme minority of market participants kill it, we will pay for it for years to come. — **J.N.**

High-frequency trading is about picking pockets— yours and mine.

ARE ALGOS GAMING GOVERNMENT REPORTS?

Great work by CNBC's Eamon Javers (@EamonJavers) on trading ahead of jobs reports, consumer-confidence data, energy numbers, and other critical releases. For the past couple months I had been scouring data, our data as well as that of my friends at Nanex, to see if we saw evidence of someone or a coordinated group of someone's trading ahead of these releases.

After hours and hours of data mining we did find some interesting clues. Specifically, it appeared, as Eamon reported this morning, that certain IP addresses were pinging servers to slow the data released from those servers. The obvious purpose of such an attack would be to gain advantage for milliseconds, perhaps even just nanoseconds.

I understand most of you don't really know or care about time frames this fast, but to give some perspective, one millisecond is one million nanoseconds. When people can trade this fast a few milliseconds of latency that they can create can be millions of nanoseconds to buy or sell futures, stocks or options. It's like letting Usain Bolt race against a turtle!

It would appear that something Eric Hunsader of Nanex refers to as a "disruptor algo" hit the market just as the Consumer Confidence numbers were being released and caused that latency, or slowed dissemination of the data to the rest of the world.

Now given that you know that 1 millisecond is 1 million nanoseconds, you can have an appreciation for how long a 50 millisecond disruption can be in nanosecond terms. Give a high frequency trading (HFT) firm a 50 million nanosecond advantage and it's pretty much game, set, match.

The chart shows big simultaneous sales in S&P Electronic futures as well as SPY, IWM, QQQ about 50 milliseconds before news release. We note that options traffic was likewise heavy, so much so that the ISE pretty much went dark for a full 1/2 second.

From what Eamon can tell me, investigators have the IP addresses of several of the firms that have been responsible for creating that unfair advantage for themselves. I suspect that variations of the "disruptor algo" will reappear this year, but let's hope the regulators give these and future pickpockets more than just a slap on the wrist.

At the time, Nanex produced a graphic that showed the impact in milliseconds of 1,500 March eMini futures hitting the SPY 50 milliseconds before the "official release". As the trader(s) hit futures and equities simultaneously (and it takes roughly 14 milliseconds for the orders to travel 790 miles), these trades appear to be evidence that millions of dollars were made on that 50 millisecond edge. — J.N.

By slowing the release of data to others, traders gained an unfair advantage.

IT'S SAFER TO TRADE FROM HOME

If you've ever seen movies like "Trading Places" or the original "Wall Street," you might get a sense of how insane things can get on the trading floor. But what they didn't show you was how rough things could get off-camera, in real life.

Every once in awhile when tempers flared in a pit, you'd hear somebody yell, "Let's go to the horse!" That referred to a statue of a horse outside the Chicago Board of Trade building, where guys would go to settle their differences.

You'd always know when this was happening because you'd see traders walking off the floor, followed by a crowd of others like some kind of pied pipers. But the group wasn't going just to watch a fight—like true traders, they were going to make a market of their own on the contest, giving odds and placing bets on the outcome. It wasn't unusual to hear things like, "I'll take 3 to 1 that Jimmy will throw the first punch."

In fact, these instances became so frequent that the CBOE created a committee to essentially police the traders, and I was asked to join it. We came up with rules ranging from a modest fine for disrupting trading by "going to the horse" to a $5,000 penalty for landing a haymaker while still in the pits.

But to be honest, I was not a big finer as a floor official. As a trader myself, I knew that sometimes things just had to be settled this way. Right or wrong, that's just the way things were in those days: It was the law of the jungle, and only the fittest survived. — **P.N.**

*Electronic trading
is a long way from
the law of the jungle.*

PART THREE:
Core Concepts

WHY WE USE OPTIONS

Trading stocks is reasonably easy, at least in theory. If you think a stock is going up, buy it. If you think it is going down, sell it; or sell it short if you are a real risk-taker. If you think a stock is going nowhere, sell it or avoid it in the first place. The stock price is what it is and that is what you pay. Things are not so simple with options trading. Many factors influence the value of an option contract. It is for largely that reason that most retail options traders underestimate the challenge of making money with options.

> *Would you like to...*
> • Increase your leverage without paying margin rates?
> • Profit from dropping prices - with limited risk?
> • Generate more income in your account?
> • Get paid to enter long stock positions?
> • Insure your positions or even your whole portfolio?

Options are exceptionally versatile. You can do all of the above with the use of options.

The Fine Print

An option is a standardized contract providing for the right - but not the obligation - to buy or sell an underlying financial instrument. In our context, this underlying is a stock or index (exchange traded fund, or ETF). The contract controls 100 shares, and is good until a defined expiration date. The price at which shares can be bought or sold also is defined by the contract, and is known as the strike price.

There are two types of options: calls and puts. You can buy or sell either type. If you buy an option you are the holder of the contract and considered to be "long," while if you sell an option you are the "writer" of the contract and considered to be "short."

The buyer of a call has the right to buy the underlying security (e.g. 100 shares of Google) at the strike price on or before the expiration date. The seller of a call has the obligation to sell the shares, if asked.

The buyer of a put has the right to sell the underlying security (e.g. 100 shares of Google) at the strike price on or before the expiration date. The seller of a put has the obligation to buy the shares, if assigned.

	Holder (Buyer)	Writer (Seller)
Call Option	Right to Buy	Obligation to Sell
Put Option	Right to Sell	Obligation to Buy

The sides of a trade

Option Price and Value Premium

In exchange for the right to buy (call) or sell (put) an underlying security on or before the expiration date, the purchaser of an option pays a premium. The price of the contract is known as the debit, and it is the purchaser's maximum risk. On the other side of the trade, the seller of the option receives the premium as a credit to his/her brokerage account, but is obligated to buy (in the case of a short put) or sell (in the instance of a short call) the underlying shares if the purchaser exercises the contract. Brokerages hold cash from the premium as a guarantee against short positions.

The strike price, or exercise price, of an option determines whether that contract is in-the-money, at-the-money, or out-of-the-money. If the strike price of a call option is less than the current market price of the underlying security, the call is said to be in-the-money because the holder of the call has the right to buy the stock at a price which is less than the price he would have to pay to buy the stock in the market. Likewise, if a put option has a strike price that is greater than the current market price of the underlying security, it is also said to be in-the-money because the holder of this put has the right to sell the stock at a price which is greater than the price he would receive in the market. The converse of in-the-money is, not surprisingly, out-of-the-money. If the strike price equals the current market price, the option is said to be at-the-money.

	Call	Put
In-the-Money (ITM)	Strike Price < Stock Price	Strike Price > Stock Price
At-the-Money (ATM)	Strike Price = Stock Price	Strike Price = Stock Price
Out-of-the-Money (OTM)	Strike Price > Stock Price	Strike Price < Stock Price

Where the money is

Intrinsic Value and Time Value

The premium of an option has two components, intrinsic value and time value. Intrinsic value describes the amount the stock price is above the strike price (for calls), or below the strike price (for puts). Therefore the amount by which an option is in-the-money is intrinsic value. It is also the value of the contract at expiration.

Time value is defined as the option premium minus the intrinsic value. It is the amount that you pay for the possibility that it will be worth more in the future. Therefore an at-the money or out-of-the-money option has no intrinsic value and only time value.

Calls	Puts
Intrinsic Value = Stock Price - Strike Price	Intrinsic Value = Strike Price - Stock Price
Time Value = Option Price - Intrinsic Value	Time Value = Option Price - Intrinsic Value

Value: time and intrinsic

Intrinsic value is only affected by moves in the underlying security.

Time value is subject to several factors, primarily time to expiration and implied volatility. Implied volatility is the market's expectation of the future volatility of the underlying stock. It is derived from the option price itself, and represents demand for the option. The higher the implied volatility, the more expectation that the underlying stock will make big moves, increasing the option's chances of being in-the-money. This also means that the option's premiums (that is, its time value) are higher. However, the value of time decays as expiration nears: time decay increases dramatically in the last 30 days as expiration approaches.

Let's consider an example using Google (GOOG). If GOOG were trading at $500 when you bought a 490 strike call option for $25, then $10 of the option's value would be intrinsic value.

The other $15 would be time value. A 500 call purchased when GOOG is trading for $500 is at-the-money, but is all time value. It has no intrinsic value.

If the stock were at $500 when you bought a 510 call, the option is again all time value, since it has to rise $10 to be at-the-money.

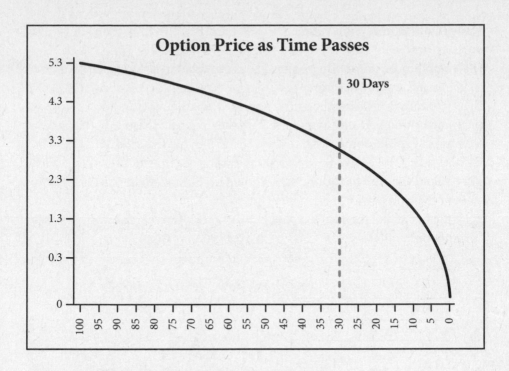

	Strike Price		
Stock Price = $500	490 Call = $25	500 Call = $18	510 Call = $10
	In the Money	At the Money	Out of the Money
	$10 Intrinsic	$0 Intrinsic	$0 Intrinsic
	$15 Time Value	$18 Time Value	$10 Time Value

Intrinsic and time value enumerated

Buying Calls

You want leverage? Buying a call gives you leverage over 100 shares of an underlying stock (or ETF) at the strike price until the expiration date. Long calls are used to profit from upward moves in the underlying.

Again using Google for an example, the GOOG December 500 call option gives you the right to buy 100 shares of GOOG for $500 per share up until the expiration date in December. You would do this with the expectation that the price of the option will rise, through the rise in the price of the underlying stock. Let's say you purchased the GOOG 500 call option for $25 when the stock was trading for $500. If GOOG goes up to $550 before expiration, then your call is worth at least $50. This gives you a 100% return on the call option based on a 10% return on the stock. That is the leverage of buying options.

The flip side is that if the stock does not move up, then the option will lose all of its value by expiration. This results from the decay of the value of the option's premium, known as time decay. That is the risk of buying calls. Since they are expiring assets, they have time value that diminishes over time. But regardless of how far the stock falls, your risk is limited to the cost of the call.

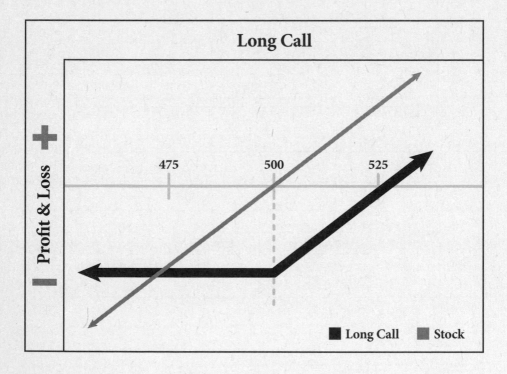

Symbol: GOOG	Stock P/L	% Return	Call P/L	% Return
$200	($300)	-60%	($25)	-100%
$500	$0	0%	($25)	-100%
$550	$50	10%	$25	100%
$600	$100	20%	$75	300%

Arithmetic of stock and a long call returns compared

Exiting Long Calls

When a call has been purchased, the position can be closed in one of three ways:

Selling the Call - Once an option is bought it can be sold at any time. This is the most common way of exiting a long position, and the only way of exiting a long call that captures any remaining time value in the option.

Letting it Expire - If a call gets all the way to expiration, it will expire worthless if it is out-of the money (when the strike price is above the stock price). If the stock price is above the strike price by $.01 or more, it will be automatically exercised and shares will be delivered to your brokerage account. Long calls are almost always sold before expiring, since at that point they will have lost all time value.

Exercising Your Call - Utilizing the "right to buy" that is inherent in the call contract is known as "exercising" the option. This results in your brokerage delivering shares of the stock to you at the strike price. Options are rarely bought with the intention of exercising the underlying right.

Buying Puts

Want to profit from the downside? Puts give the buyer the right to sell a specific number of shares (usually 100) of an underlying stock at the strike price until the expiration date. Long puts will profit if the underlying price falls, all else held equal. Buying puts therefore offers a limited-risk way to profit from the downside. This also makes them a way to protect positions as insurance (see the lesson on Protective Puts).

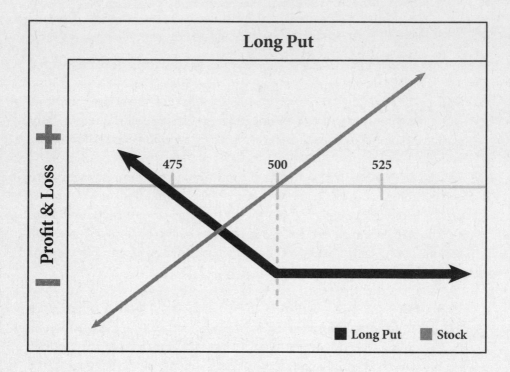

In this case, let's say you were concerned about the downside, so you purchased the GOOG 500 put option for $25 when GOOG the stock was trading for $500. If GOOG goes down to $450 before expiration, then your put is worth at least $50. This gives you a 100% return on the put option with a 10% loss on the stock.

Symbol: GOOG	Stock P/L	% Return	Put P/L	% Return
$400	($100)	-20%	$75	300%
$450	($50)	-10%	$25	100%
$500	$0	0%	($25)	-100%
$600	$100	20%	($25)	-100%

Arithmetic of stock and a long put returns compared

Buying puts on a stock you own can provide insurance on that position. Index puts can also be used to insure your entire portfolio. Buying puts is very much like buying insurance. You pick the deductible and the premiums.

Exiting Long Puts

When a put has been purchased, the position can be closed in one of three ways:

Selling the Put - Once a put is bought it can be sold at any time, and this is the most common way of exiting a long position. This is the only way of exiting a long position that captures any remaining time value in the option.

Letting it Expire - If a put gets all the way to expiration, it will expire, worthless if it is out-of-the-money (when the stock price is above the strike price - See Options Pricing). If the stock price is below the strike price by $.01 or more, it will be automatically exercised and shares will be "taken" from your brokerage account. Long options are almost always sold before expiring, as at that point they will have lost all time value.

Exercising the Option - Utilizing the "right to sell" that is inherent in the put contract is known as exercising the option. This delivers shares of the stock from your account at the strike price. Options are rarely bought with the intention of exercising the underlying right. Taking this course also forgoes any remaining time value in the option.

Rules for Buying

Regardless of whether you are buying calls or puts, there are some general rules to follow.

One, the expiration should give the option enough time to perform without being overexposed to time decay. Since options have an expiration date, a large part of their value is time value (for more, see our lesson on Options Pricing). This time value will deteriorate as that expiration approaches; time decay increases exponentially in the last 30 to 45 days of an options life, so this is usually not the time to own options.

Two, options should generally be bought when implied volatility, or the expected price swings of the underlying, is expected to stay flat or to rise. Buying options is a limited-risk strategy, and all of that risk lies in the premium paid for the option. All else equal, if there is a rise in implied volatility, then there will be a rise in the option premiums. This increase can produce profits for long options, even if the stock price doesn't move, because the chance of movement has increased. Conversely, if you buy options when implied volatility and premiums are high, such as before earnings, then the stock can move in the direction that you want and you can still lose money, because with the news out, the implied volatility generally falls.

Finally, when you buy an option, generally you will want to sell it, ideally for a still-greater premium. You do not want it to expire, since you will receive zero premium, and normally you don't want to exercise your right to purchase the underlying shares, unless that is your particular strategy (say for tax reasons).

In both of these cases, you lose whatever time value is left in the option. So with future resale value in mind, we can see why risk management rules are important, such as taking profits when your position doubles or closing out the position when it loses half of their entry value.

Selling Calls

Interested in generating income? When option premiums are high (that is, when implied volatility is high), some traders turn to selling options. Selling "naked" calls, so called because you do not own the underlying shares as a hedge in case you are assigned, is a neutral to bearish strategy. You want the market price to be below the strike of the call you sold, so that it expires worthless. Selling calls should be done when you expect the underlying stock to fall or stay flat.

Option buyers have rights, but option sellers have obligations. By selling calls, you are obligating yourself to selling the stock at the strike price when you are assigned. Assignment is the other side of an option being exercised. If a call buyer decides to exercise the long call, that exercise is put out randomly to a seller—any seller—of that call, and the individual is obligated to sell stock to the call buyer.

If you do not own the shares of the stock when assigned, then you will have to come up with them. This is the reason that brokerages require a margin account for individuals who wish to sell naked calls. It is also the reason that selling calls is considered the options strategy with the highest risk. Stocks can go up infinitely, and so the risk of a naked call is unlimited. Naked calls are the strategy that gives options a bad name among the risk averse.

By way of explanation, let's say you sold the GOOG 500 call option for $25 when GOOG was trading for $500. If GOOG is anywhere below $500 at expiration, then you keep your credit of $25. If the stock goes up to $525, however, you will be assigned at expiration, but will come out flat since you already pocketed a credit of $25. As the stock price continues upward, your losses mount.

Symbol: GOOG	Stock P/L	% Return	Call P/L
$300	($200)	-40%	$25
$500	$0	0%	$25
$550	$50	10%	($25)
$700	$200	40%	($175)

Arithmetic of stock and a short call returns compared

Because of this unlimited risk as the underlying stock price rises, selling calls is rarely done in isolation. In fact, selling calls against stock that you own, known as "covered calls" or "buy-writes," is considered by many the most conservative options strategy. (For more, see the lesson on Covered Calls.)

Selling Puts

Want to be paid to buy stock? Many stock investors use "limit orders" to get into long positions. Another way to buy stock for less than the current market price is an options strategy called cash-secured puts. Cash secured means that you have the cash in your account to buy the stock at the designated strike price. Selling puts is usually done with options that have high implied volatility. This is a neutral to bullish strategy which can be used to generate income, or to enter long stock positions.

Selling puts obligates you to buy the stock if assigned. This strategy brings income into your account, which is your profit if the stock is above the strike price at expiration. Traders sell puts if they think the stock is going to stay flat or go up slightly, but only if they are willing to buy the stock if assigned. For this reason, selling puts can be an excellent way to initiate long stock positions, and get paid to do so.

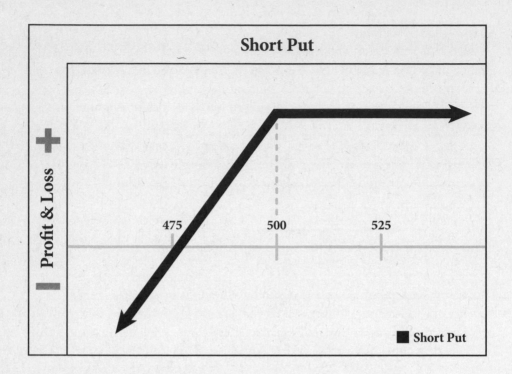

Symbol: GOOG	Stock P/L	% Return	Put P/L
$300	($200)	-40%	($175)
$450	$0	0%	($25)
$500	$50	10%	$25
$700	$200	40%	$25

Arithmetic of stock and a short put returns compared

Let's say you sold the GOOG 500 put option for $25 when the stock was trading for $500. If GOOG is anywhere above $500 at expiration, then you keep your credit of $25. If the stock is below, you will be assigned, and you will purchase the stock at the strike price. But the trade itself is profitable until $475, since you pocketed the $25 credit.

Puts can be sold cash-secured or naked. If they are cash secured, then you have the cash in your account to purchase the stock at the strike price if assigned. If naked, then a lower margin is required. This would increase the return on margin, but also increase the potential risk.

Exiting Short Positions

When an option has been sold, the position can be closed in one of three ways:

Buying Back the Option - After an option is sold, it can be bought back at any time. This is done when there is a risk of assignment that the option seller wants to avoid. For instance, if you sold a call, the stock went up through your strike, and you do not want to be assigned and forced to sell the stock, you could buy back the option to close the position.

Letting it Expire - If the option gets all the way to expiration, it will expire, worthless if it is out-of-the-money. Typically, this is what you want to have happen with options that you have sold. If it is in-the-money by $.01, it will be automatically exercised and you will be assigned, automatically selling stock if you were short a call or buying stock if you were short a put.

Assignment - American-style options (all equity and ETF options) can be exercised at any time before expiration. So you could be assigned at any time after you have sold an option. Most traders view this as a negative, but it is not necessarily so. If you are using cash-secured puts to acquire stock, then assignment means you have achieved your objective at a below-market price.

Rules for Selling

Selling options is best done when implied volatilities, and therefore option premiums, are high and expected to fall. This is because higher implied volatility brings in more premium income to your account. It is important to remember, however, that selling options involves considerable risk, and high implied volatility can always go higher.

Since we already know that time decay is greatest in the last 30 to 45 days, this is typically the best time to sell options. The ideal is to have the options expire worthless, but we usually recommend buying back short options when they get to some minimum amount (like $.15) to limit risk. Generally speaking, if we wouldn't sell it at the time, we don't want to be short. And, unless necessary, we are not interested in buying back the options we have sold.

Review of Basic Strategies with Examples

Profit from stock price gains

Example: You buy one Cisco (CSCO) 25 call with the stock at 25, and you pay $1. CSCO moves up to $28 and so your option gains at least $2 in value, giving you a 200% gain versus a 12% increase in the stock. Profit from stock price drops with limited risk and lower cost than shorting the stock.

Profit from the downside

Example: You buy one Hewlett-Packard (HPQ) 20 put with HPQ at $21, and you pay $.80. HPQ drops to 18 and you have a gain of $1.20, which is 150%. The stock lost 10%. Profit from sideways markets by selling options and generating income.

Earn extra income

Example: You own 100 shares of Oracle (ORCL). With the stock at 34, you sell one ORCL 35 call for $1.00. If the stock is still at 34 at expiration, the option will expire worthless, and you made a 3% return on your holdings in a flat market.

Get paid to buy stock

Example: Netflix (NFLX) is trading for $175, a price you like, and you sell an at-the-money put for $9. If the stock is below $175 at expiration, you are assigned, and essentially purchase the shares for $166.

Protect positions or portfolios

Example: You own 100 shares of NFLX at $190 and want to protect your position, so you buy a NFLX 175 put for $1. Should the stock drop to $120, you are protected dollar for dollar from $174 down, and your loss is only $16, not $70.

BASIC TERMINOLOGY

Calls - The right, but not the obligation, to buy a specific number of shares of the underlying security at a defined price, until the expiration date.

Puts - The right, but not the obligation, to sell a specific number of shares of the underlying security at a defined price until the expiration date.

Strike Price - The price at which option holders can exercise their rights.

Exercise - The process in which the buyer of an option takes, or makes, delivery of the underlying contract.

Assignment - The process by which the seller of an option is notified that the contract has been exercised.

Expiration - The time at which an option can no longer be exercised.

In-the-Money (ITM) - A call (put) option whose strike price is below (above) the stock price.

At-the-Money (ATM) - An option whose strike price is roughly equal to the stock price.

Out-of-the-Money (OTM) - A call (put) option whose strike price is above (below) the stock price.

American Style - An option that can be exercised at any time before expiration.

European Style - An option that can be exercised only at expiration.
(Note: These are mainly index options.)

Intrinsic Value - The amount that an option is in-the-money.

Time Value - The price of an option less the intrinsic value.

Option Chains

For any given option contract, we need to know the most recent prices and other factors. Option chains show data for a given underlying's different strike prices and expiration months.

Option Chain for Intel Corp. (INTC)
$21.25 ▼ -0.61 (-2.79%) Volume: 57.96 M 3:23 PM EDT January 27, 2011

Option Filter: Composite ☑ All ☑ At The Money ☑ GO Help

Feb 11 Mar 11 Apr 11 May 11 Jun 11 Jul 11 Aug 11 Sep 11 Oct 11 Nov 11 Dec 11 Jan 11

Calls	Last	Chg	Bid	Ask	Vol	Open Int	Strike	Puts	Last	Chg	Bid	Ask	Vol	Open Int
@NQDV	9.19	0.14	8.75	8.85	2	824	12.50	@NQPV	0.02	-	-	0.02	1	2887
@NQDC	6.80	-	6.20	6.35	0	2355	15.00	@NQPC	0.02	-	-	0.03	0	3290
@NQDQ	5.15	-	5.20	5.40	0	1654	16.00	@NQPQ	0.01	0.04	0.01	0.03	10	1537
@NQDW	3.95	-0.50	3.80	3.90	212	7107	17.50	@NQPW	0.07	0.01	0.07	0.09	173	20597
@NQDT	2.54	-0.47	2.50	2.53	345	3953	19.00	@NQPT	0.23	0.07	0.22	0.24	124	13710
@NQDD	1.75	-0.47	1.72	1.74	2527	33593	20.00	@NQPD	0.45	0.15	0.44	0.45	2702	59325
@NQDU	1.10	-0.36	1.06	1.06	4466	23528	21.00	@NQPU	0.76	0.20	0.78	0.79	3405	28891
@NQDX	0.42	-0.23	0.41	0.41	3452	53399	22.50	@NQPX	1.64	0.41	1.63	1.64	1544	40392
@NQDB	0.12	-0.09	0.13	0.13	206	11807	24.00	@NQPB	2.74	0.51	2.82	2.86	31	27803
@JNQDE	0.06	-0.04	0.06	0.06	102	57633	25.00	@JNQPE	3.69	0.64	3.70	3.85	18	4220
@JNQDY	0.02	-	0.01	0.01	0	34576	27.50	@JNQPY	6.16	-	6.20	6.30	0	361
@JNQDF	0.01	-	-	-	66	30721	30.00	@JNQPF	9.00	-	8.70	8.80	0	30721

A typical options chain

At the top, we have the stock information and then different expiration months. In this case we are looking at Intel (INTC). Down the middle are the strike prices. Calls are on the left, puts on the right. Contracts in-the-money are gray, and out-of-the-money are white.

Each strike lists:
- The price of the last trade ("last")
- The price at which there are willing buyers (the "bid")
- The price at which a contract is offered for sale (the "ask" or "offer")
- The volume of the day's trading ("vol")
- The contract's "open interest" ("open int" or "oi"), which tells us how many active contracts there are for a given month and strike.

High open interest figures, generally near the at-the-money strikes, tell us there are more prospective trading partners who could accept your price. But note that volume does not equal open interest, since some trades are made to close positions.

SUMMARY

- Options are used for speculation, income generation, or hedging a position.

- Options buyers pay a premium for the right to, not the obligation, to act.

- Options sellers (writers) have an obligation (if assigned).

- There are four basic positions: buying calls, buying puts, selling calls, and selling puts.

- Option premiums are made up of intrinsic value and time value.

- Time value is largely a function of implied volatility.

LONG CALLS

Would you like to...
• Have more leverage without increasing use of margin?
• Have a low-capital, low-risk way of profiting from rising stock prices?

You think XYZ stock is going to go up in the near future. You don't really want to tie up all the capital necessary to profit, and you don't want to pay margin rates. But you still want leverage. As one top hedge fund manager said, "the only way most people really do well in the markets is to be long and leveraged". Buying calls is the best way to be "long and leveraged".

Buying calls is the one options strategy most every option trader has executed. Calls are a bet on the rise in price of the underlying stock. This is the option strategy that is most like buying stocks, and so is a popular entry into options trading. Calls are a limited-risk way to profit from rising prices in the underlying, and thus provide for leveraged speculation.

What is a Long Call?

Buying calls gives you the ability to control a lot of stock without owning it, or "leverage." Equity calls give the buyer the right to buy 100 shares of an underlying stock or exchange traded funds (ETFs) at a designated strike price until the expiration date. Long calls are used to profit from upward moves in the underlying.

Buying calls is as simple as picking the strike and expiration date that you wish to buy. Call buyers often use out-of-the-money options (when the strike is above the stock price) because they are "cheap" and appear to offer the best leverage. Speculators and traders must keep in mind, however, that out-of-the-money options also offer a lower probability of profit.

Long calls have significant profit potential, as holders generally will make money as the stock moves up. Because you are paying a premium, in essence buying time value, the stock has to rise above the strike price plus the cost of the contract to be profitable at expiration. Significant upward price moves will benefit the position. Long calls also benefit from an increase in implied volatility (because the likelihood of movement, which is implied by the price of the option, is the key component of the time value of the option contract's price). Option buyers are best served by divesting their long positions as expiration gets close, however, as that is when time decay is greatest.

The long call strategy loses if the stock price, at expiration, is below the strike price plus the premium paid. The maximum risk is the amount paid for the call. Clearly if the underlying price falls, the position will lose value. If the implied volatility drops (thus lowering the time value of the option), the position can also lose value, even if the underlying moves up. This is the reason that buying calls before earnings (or other news) can be a risky strategy. Even if the stock moves up, the drop in implied volatility that often happens after earnings are released can more than offset the gain from the move in the underlying.

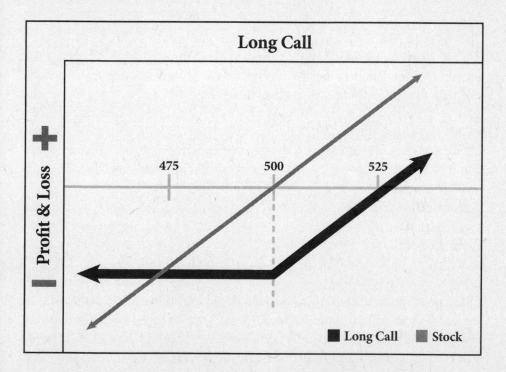

Example: You purchase the GOOG 500 call option for $25 while Google stock is trading for $500. If GOOG goes up to $550 before expiration, then your call will be worth at least $50. This gives you a 100% return on the call option (before counting the cost of the option) with just a 10% gain on the stock. That is what is meant by the leverage of buying options.

The flip side is that if the stock does not move up, then the option will lose all of its value by expiration. This is the result of the decay of the premium of the option, known as time decay. That is the risk of buying calls. Since they are expiring assets, they have time value that diminishes over time. But regardless of how far the stock falls, your risk is limited to the cost of the call.

Symbol: GOOG	Stock P/L	% Return	Call P/L	% Return
$200	($300)	-60%	($25)	-100%
$500	$0	0%	($25)	-100%
$550	$50	10%	$25	100%
$600	$100	20%	$75	300%

Arithmetic of stock and a long call returns compared

The long call will profit from the stock price rising, all else held equal. The position will lose as the stock price moves down, but that loss is capped at the $25 paid for the position. Because implied volatility is a significant part of the premium paid for an option, if implied volatility goes down, the long call will lose value, and if implied volatility goes up, it will gain. This is only the case before expiration, because at expiration profit and loss is fixed. Time is against you with a long call, so every day you are losing value from time decay.

Rules for Buying

Regardless of whether you are buying calls or puts, there are some general rules to follow.

One, the expiration should give the option enough time to perform without being overexposed to time decay. Since options have an expiration date, a large part of their value is time value (for more, see our lesson on Options Pricing). This time value will deteriorate as that expiration approaches; time decay increases exponentially in the last 30 to 45 days of an options life, so this is usually not the time to own options.

Two, options should generally be bought when the implied volatility, or the expected price swings of the underlying - is expected to stay flat or to rise. Buying options is a limited-risk strategy, and all of that risk lies in the premium paid for the option. If there is a rise in implied volatility, then there will be a rise in the option premiums. This increase can produce profits for long

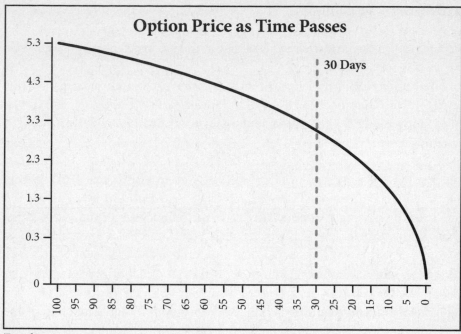

Time decay

options, even if the stock price doesn't move, because the chance of movement has increased.

Conversely, if you buy options when implied volatility and premiums are high, such as before earnings, then the stock can move in the direction that you want and you can still lose money, because with the news out, the implied volatility could fall.

Finally, when you buy an option, generally you will want to sell it, ideally for a still-greater premium. You do not want it to expire, since you will receive zero premium, and normally you don't want to exercise your right to purchase the underlying shares, unless that is your particular strategy (say for tax reasons).

In both of these cases, you lose whatever time value is left in the option. So with future resale value in mind, we can see why risk management rules are important, such as taking profits when your position doubles or closing out the position when it loses half of their entry value.

Exiting Long Calls

When a call has been purchased, the position can be closed in one of three ways:

Selling the Call - Once an option is bought it can be sold at any time. This is the most common way of exiting a long position, and the only way of exiting a long call that allows one to capture any remaining time value in the option.

Letting it Expire - If a call gets all the way to expiration, it will expire, worthless if it is out-of-the-money (when the strike price is above the stock price - see Options Pricing). If the stock price is above the strike price by $.01 or more, it will be automatically exercised and shares will be delivered to your brokerage account. Long calls are almost always sold before expiring, as at that point they will have lost all time value.

Exercising your Call - Utilizing the "right to buy" that is inherent in the call contract is known as exercising the option. This delivers shares of the stock to you at the strike price. Options are rarely bought with the intention of exercising the underlying right. Taking this course also forgoes any remaining time value in the option.

Example of a Winning Trade

In the circled area (next page), the price of Intel (INTC) bounces off a low while implied volatilities, and hence option premiums, stay low. Ideally we want to buy calls on low implied volatility because that means that there is less time decay working against us.

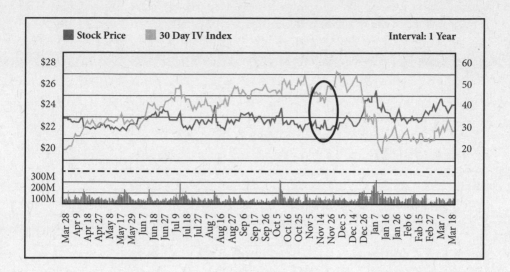

Time decay is the greatest in the last month before expiration, so in this case, with the stock climbing back above $25 and implied volatility at 30%, we would buy three months out, February 27.5 calls for $.70.

If the underlying price rises, and implied volatility does not drop (as was the case), it is best to sell the call and not hold it all the way to expiration, thereby losing any time value.

In this case, the stock hit $28 within two weeks and implied volatility went to 34%. The option went from $.70 to $2.10.

Using disciplined position management, we would have exited this position before the full gain, taking half of the position off after a 100% gain, selling most of the rest at a 200% gain. The reason to do so is to avoid letting a winner become a loser, since we couldn't have known the future trajectory of the option.

Example of a Losing Trade

Three things can go against us when buying calls: underlying direction, implied volatility, and time.

Using the same underlying as on the previous page, if we had bought calls a month earlier, the trade might not have worked out as well. In the highlighted area we see INTC breaking out to a new high. But most options traders ignore implied volatility and buy out-of-the-money calls only in the near months. So with the stock at $26.50 and the implied volatility at 41%, we could have bought the November 27 call for $1.10.

The price did move up to $27.50, but with time decay and the drop in implied volatility, the position showed a loss, with the value drooping to $.99. The price then fell further and took the option price down to $.55, where our 50% stop-loss limit would have been hit and we would exit the trade.

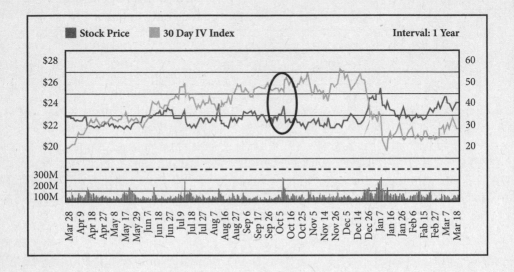

SUMMARY

- Long calls are a bullish position.

- They can be a limited-risk, leveraged way to profit from rising prices in the underlying.

- They are significantly affected by implied volatility and time decay.

- The maximum risk is limited, while the maximum gain is unlimited.

COVERED CALLS

Would you like to...
- Generate income in neutral or rising markets?
- Get paid to sell your long stock position?

You own a stock that is part of your long-term investment portfolio. You like it long term, but don't see it going anywhere over the short term and would consider selling it, given the right terms. You would also like to generate some income, but you aren't interested in selling your stock only to buy a CD with a next-to-nothing return.

Given these conditions, many self-directed (or "retail") traders use covered calls to generate income in their accounts. It is considered to be highly conservative and is therefore widely popular. In fact, many stock traders begin trading options this way. The strategy can also be used to offset a small part of the cost of purchasing long stock positions. This approach is known as a "buy-write," when the investor buys the stock and writes (or sells) the call. A covered call is equivalent to a cash-secured put.

What is a Covered Call?

Implementing the covered call strategy involves buying (or owning) 100 shares of a stock and then selling a call that is "covered" by the stock (since 1 option contract usually controls 100 shares of stock). The sale is a credit and adds cash to your account. But while selling the call brings income to the account, it creates the obligation to sell the stock if the call is assigned. Note that this can create tax issues for stock, especially those with a low cost basis.

Covered calls are profitable within a defined range. They profit if the stock price drops by less than the amount of the sold call, and remain profitable if the stock moves up to or beyond the strike price of the call sold. The maximum gain is realized if the stock price is at the strike price. At that point, the full value of the sold call is retained while the stock has achieved its maximum without assignment.

Example: With the stock at $48, you sell a 50 call for $1. If the stock goes to $49.50, you gain $1.50 per share and keep the $1 of premium.

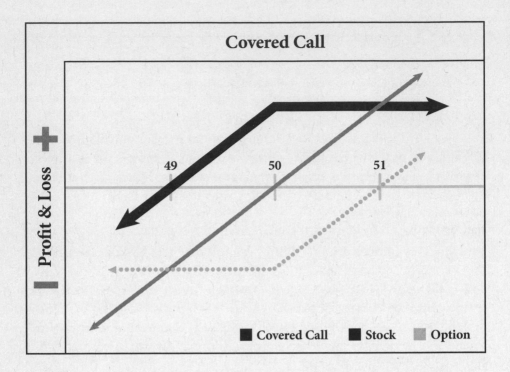

If the stock goes to $47.20, there is .20 of profit. Your stock would have lost $.80, but you gained $1 from selling the call option. Meanwhile, if the stock goes to $50.30 at expiration, the call will be assigned and the stock sold. You will recognize a $2.00 gain in the stock price and $1 profit from the option premium which you received; but of course you will have sold your stock. If the sold call can be bought back for a small amount before expiration, it's best to do so, in order to lock in your profit and eliminate exposure to risk.

This strategy loses if the stock price drops significantly. To exit a position, you will need to first buy back the call and then sell the stock. In a falling market,

Symbol: XYZ	Stock P/L	Call P/L	Covered Call P/L
$40	($8)	$1	($7)
$47	($1)	$1	$0
$50	$2	$1	$3
$60	$12	($9)	$3

Arithmetic of stock and covered call returns compared

this can be problematic. The credit from selling the call gives you small cushion, but not real downside protection.

Alternately, if the stock takes off and moves beyond the strike price sold, the position will not partake in those gains. You still make a profit, but there is the possibility of assignment before expiration. If you are assigned, you will have to sell your stock, which can create tax issues (especially if you have held the stock for a long time). If the stock price is above the strike price at expiration, you will be assigned.

To reiterate, the covered call will profit from the stock's moving up, staying flat, or falling no more than the credit from the sold call. The position will lose as the stock price moves down beyond the amount of the credit. Because implied volatility (the volatility expectation taken from the options price) is a significant part of the premium paid for an option, if implied volatility goes down, the covered call will profit, and if implied volatility goes up, it will lose. This is only the case before expiration, because at expiration profit and loss is fixed. Time is on your side with a covered call. You have a position with positive theta and so every day you are profiting from time decay (all else held equal).

Example of a Winning Trade

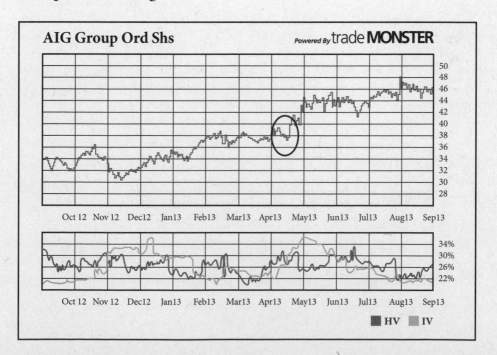

In mid-April, AIG dipped to support at $38, putting in a higher low after a higher high. At the same time implied volatility hit an eight-month high around 39%. We want to sell calls on high implied volatility because that is more premium and time decay in our favor.

Time decay is the greatest in the front month, so in this case, with the stock at 38.5 and rising, we would sell one month out: May 40.5 calls for $1.

If the underlying prices falls, and/or implied volatility drops (as is the case), it is usually best to buy back the call at some pre-determined value (say $.15).

As it happened, implied volatility held up for a couple of weeks before dropping to 24%. The stock price quickly rose above $41 and then $44. So in this case it is likely best to wait for expiration and assignment, or we could close out the calls and stock together as one trade. If we had waited, we would have had the $1 profit from the option and $2 from the rise in the stock price, a gain of almost 8% for the month (minus commissions and fees).

Example of a Losing Trade

Some people like to use ETFs (exchange traded funds) for covered calls to minimize risk, but that doesn't mean that there isn't any risk. Here is an example using the QQQ.

Here, in late October, we seemed to have the price bottoming out, with a spike in implied volatility. With the price at $65 and the implied volatility up to 21, we sell the November 67 call for $0.80.

The rebound doesn't happen, and the price dives down to $62 as the implied volatility holds steady. Now we have two options. If we decide that we want to get out of the entire position, then we need to first buy back the call, and then sell the stock. Otherwise we can wait until expiration if we think that the QQQ will be back up above $64.20 (our break-even point) by expiration.

We hold the position and stock is down around $62 at expiration, so we have a loss, but it is reduced by the amount of the credit of the sold call.

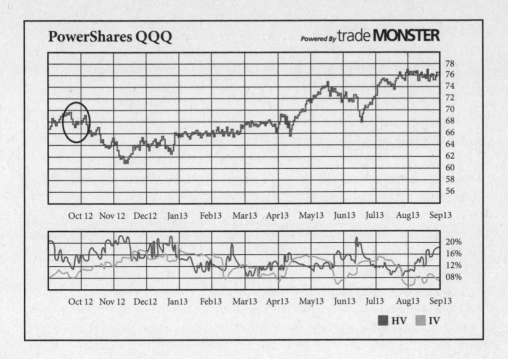

SUMMARY

- The covered call strategy involves owning or buying stock and selling calls against it in a 1-to-1 ratio.

- It is a slightly bullish to neutral strategy.

- It can generate extra income in your account and potentially reduce volatility.

- It is equivalent to a short put.

- The maximum gain is limited; the risk is the same as owning the stock (minus the credit for selling the calls).

PROTECTIVE PUTS

Would you like to...
- Have a limited-risk way of profiting from falling stock prices?
- Be able to buy insurance on your stocks or overall portfolio?

You insure your house. You insure your car. Why don't you insure your portfolio?

Insurance for your portfolio—or most stock positions—is available using put options. While options have the reputation of being risky assets in some circles, their original purpose was as insurance policies to protect positions, and buying puts is a limited risk way of doing just that.

What is a Protective Put?

Puts make money when the underlying stock goes down, and therefore when owned along with the underlying, provide downside protection. As a buyer you limit the risk of stock ownership. Just as with your other insurance policies, your risk is the premium you pay. And like your other insurance policies, you have it in place with the intention of not using it.

A protective put requires you to identify the strike price and the expiration date that you want, and to purchase the option. This is as easy as picking a stop-loss point, usually involving an out-of-the-money put (a put strike that is below the stock price) which restricts the loss to a size that you are comfortable with. Add the cost of the option to the difference between the stock price and the strike price, and that is your maximum loss to the downside. And for those stock traders familiar with stop-losses, there is no slippage and no "flash crashes" down past your stop price.

As options are expiring assets, they are also decaying assets. There is a time value component to the premium price of an option and every day that amount decreases. The decay rate also increases as expiration approaches. Longer-term options decay at slower rates than short-term options, so most investors use longer term puts for protection, and sell them before the decay rate increases dramatically (usually in the last 30 to 45 days).

For example, if you own 100 shares of EBAY at $31.00 and want to protect your position, you could buy a four-month 30 strike put for $2. Below $28 (the strike minus the premium cost of the option), you are protected dollar for dollar against stock declines.

We can see that EBAY would have to drop all the way to $28 to produce the maximum loss of $300. An increase in implied volatility would help the position and therefore would lower that price at which the maximum loss occurs.

If the stock moves up to $36, a gain of $300 is produced. Again this will be impacted by a rise or fall in implied volatility.

Finally, if the stock remains unchanged, time decay will eat away at the options value and will produce a small loss (the cost of insurance).

Rules for Buying

Whether you are buying calls or puts, there are some general rules:

One, the expiration should give the option enough time to perform without being overexposed to time decay. Since options have an expiration date, a large part of their value is time value (for more, see our lesson on Options Pricing). This time value will deteriorate as that expiration approaches; time decay increases exponentially in the last 30 to 45 days of an options life, so this is usually not the time to own options.

Two, options should generally be bought when implied volatility, or the expected price swings of the underlying, is expected to stay flat or to rise. Buying options is a limited-risk strategy, and all of that risk lies in the premium paid for the option. If there is a rise in implied volatility, then there will be a rise in the option premiums. This increase can produce profits for long options, even if the stock price doesn't move, because the expectation of movement has increased. Conversely, if you buy options when implied volatility and premiums are high, such as before earnings, then the stock can move in the direction that you want and you can still lose money, because with the news out, the implied volatility could fall.

Three, when you buy an option, generally you will want to sell it, ideally for a still-greater premium. You do not want it to expire, since you will receive zero premium, and normally you don't want to exercise your right to purchase the underlying shares, unless that is your particular strategy (say for tax reasons).

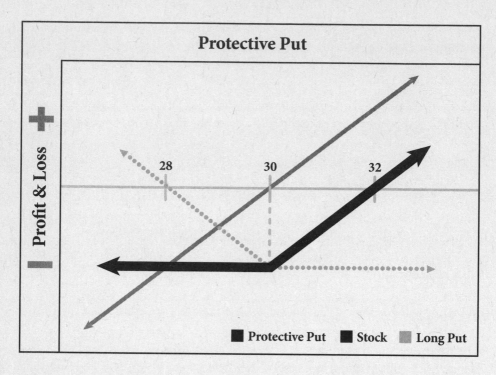

In both of these cases, you lose whatever time value is left in the option. So with future resale value in mind, we can see why risk management rules are important, such as taking profits when your position doubles or closing out the position when it loses half of their entry value.

Stock Price	Stock Gain/Loss	Put Gain/Loss	Total Gain/Loss
$36	$5	($2)	$3
$31	$0	($2)	($2)
$28	($3)	$0	($3)
$25	($6)	$3	($3)

Arithmetic of stock and protective put returns compared

Exiting Long Puts

When a put has been purchased, the position can be closed in one of three ways:

Selling the Put - Once a put is bought it can be sold at any time, and this is the most common way of exiting a long position. This is the only way of exiting a long position that captures any remaining time value in the option.

Letting it Expire - If a put gets all the way to expiration, it will expire, worthless if it is out-of-the-money (when the stock price is above the strike price - See Options Pricing). If the stock price is below the strike price by $.01 or more, it will be automatically exercised and shares will be "taken" from your brokerage account. Long options are almost always sold before expiring, as at that point they will have lost all time value.

Exercising the Option - Utilizing the "right to sell" that is inherent in the put contract is known as exercising the option. This delivers shares of the stock from your account at the strike price. Options are rarely bought with the intention of exercising the underlying right. Taking this course also forgoes any remaining time value in the option.

Example of a Winning Trade

On May 17, the QQQ price hit a multi-year high at the same time that implied volatility bottomed. Ideally we want to buy puts on low implied volatility because that means lower premiums and lower time decay, which is in our favor.

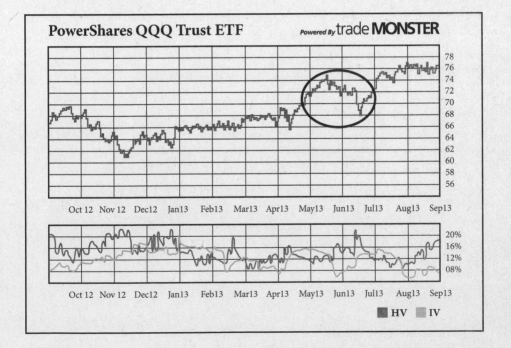

Time decay is the greatest in the front month and for strikes near the money, so with the stock hitting resistance at $74 and implied volatility at 13 we would buy 2 to 3 months out, in this case the August 72 puts for $.75.

If the underlying price falls, and implied volatility rises (as was the case), the put protection kicks in.

The stock hit $69 by June and implied volatility went almost to 20. The option went from $.75 to $4.05 even with a month of time decay, providing the protection we desired.

Using disciplined position management, we would have kept the put on and exited only if we felt the stock had hit a new support level and was holding that support with a high probability of bouncing back up. This would have allowed us to hold onto the long position through the sell-off, because our put offset much of our loss.

When the stock starts to recover in late June, we could have taken the put off at a profit and begun to ride the stock back up. In this case, QQQ traded up higher than where we originally established our put, trading up to $77 by the beginning of August. The put bought us time to weather the sell-off, allowing us to hold the position long enough to take advantage of the stock's breaking through the old $74 resistance and proceeding to new highs.

Example of a Losing Trade

What you don't want with protective puts is a sideways market, especially if implied volatility falls. Using the same underlying, if we had bought puts in mid to late January, the trade might not have worked out as well. In the highlighted area we see the QQQ jumping higher and implied volatility back down to 15 level.

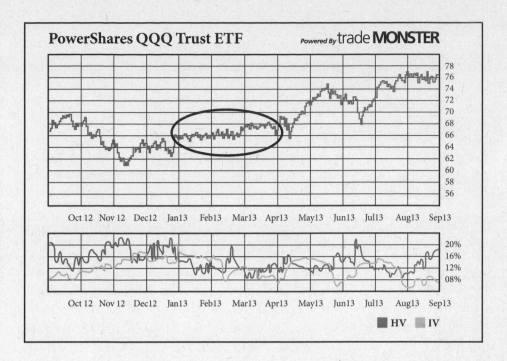

So with the ETF at $67.25 and the implied volatility at 15, we could have bought the March 64 put for $.70.

The position showed a small profit after two weeks as the price dropped and IV went up. But then both reversed. The price went up and was at $67.75 at the expiration, and the implied volatility dropped a bit. So we made no money on the price direction and we lost money on the protective put.

SUMMARY

- Long puts can be used to protect holdings or portfolios as insurance.

- They can be a limited-risk way to profit from downside moves in the underlying.

- They are significantly affected by implied volatility and time decay.

- When long puts are used as protection for a stock holding, the combination is equivalent to a long call.

- The maximum risk is capped; the maximum gain is unlimited to the upside.

SHORT PUTS

Would you like to...
- Generate income in neutral to rising markets?
- Get paid to enter "limit buy" orders for a stock you would like to own?

Many retail traders use short puts to generate income in their accounts. Short puts can also be an excellent way to acquire stock. The position is very similar to a covered call.

What is a Short Put?

Selling puts are often seen as a way to make money in a neutral market. Having chosen the strike and expiration date of an options contract, your sale is a credit and adds cash to your account. If the short put is "cash secured," which is often prudent, it means you to have enough cash in your account to purchase the stock at the designated strike. For instance, if you sold a 30 put for $1, you would have $3,000 cash in your account, in order to buy 100 shares of stock for $30 if assigned. *(Note: Your broker may require short puts to be cash secured, or may have different margin requirements.)*

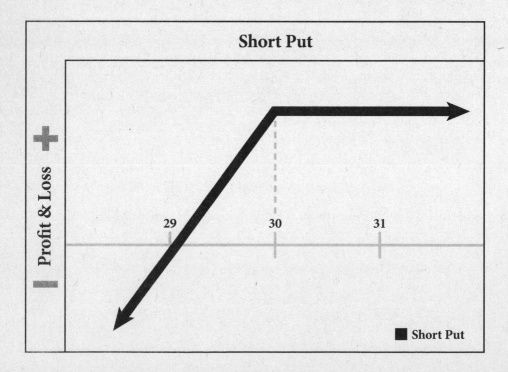

Short puts profit by the amount of the credit if the stock is above the strike price at expiration: The maximum profit is the credit that you took into your account.

For example, with the stock at $31, let's say you sold the 30 put for $1. You get to keep your $1 credit if at expiration the stock is anywhere above 30. If the stock is at $29.50 at expiration, you will have made $.50, but you also will be assigned and have to purchase the stock. (This is why it's advisable to secure the put with cash.) The strategy is actually profitable down to $29, since you did get a credit. Most traders close out the position prior to expiration if they can buy back the option for a much lower price than they sold it, for instance selling the put for $1.00, and buying back for $.15.

Symbol: XYZ	Stock P/L	Short Put P/L
$24	($7)	($5)
$29	($2)	$0
$31	$0	$1
$35	$4	$1

Arithmetic of stock and short put returns compared

As you can see, using cash-secured puts can be a way to get paid to enter a limit order. In the case above, if you want to buy the stock for $30, and the stock is trading at $31, you can sell the 30 put for $1. If the stock is below $30 at expiration you will buy the stock at $30, but because of the credit, you really only pay $29.

This strategy loses if the stock price drops significantly. Below the strike price that you sold, you have the same risk as owning the stock, because essentially you do.

The value of a short put position will profit from the stock moving up, as the put loses value. The position will lose as the stock price moves down. Because implied volatility is a significant part of the premium paid for an option, if implied volatility goes down, the short put will profit and if implied volatility goes up, it will lose. Of course, this is only the case before expiration, because at expiration profit and loss is fixed. Time is on your side with a short put. You have a position with positive theta and so every day you are profiting from time decay (as long as the stock price doesn't drop significantly).

There are several potential advantages in selling cash-secured puts to covered calls. The first is that you pay one commission as opposed to two. (This assumes that you are not assigned, and don't incur the fees that would come with assignment.) Risk management is typically easier with the one position. Puts also usually command higher premiums than calls and therefore offer better potential returns. The best way to analyze this is by using the comparative implied volatilities.

Let's look at a real world example. Let's say the XLF (a financial sector Exchange Traded Fund) is trading at $24.98 (which is as close to at-the-money of the 25 strike as you are going to get in reality). The 25 call is selling for $1.36 and the 25 put is selling for $1.52. Going out-of-the-money one strike, the 30 call is selling for $.89 and the 20 put is selling for $1.08. Clearly the return is better in both cases selling the put.

Example of a Winning Trade

In mid-April, AIG dipped to support at $38, putting in a higher low after a higher high. At the same time implied volatility hit an eight-month high around 39%. We want to sell puts on high implied volatility because that is more premium and time decay in our favor.

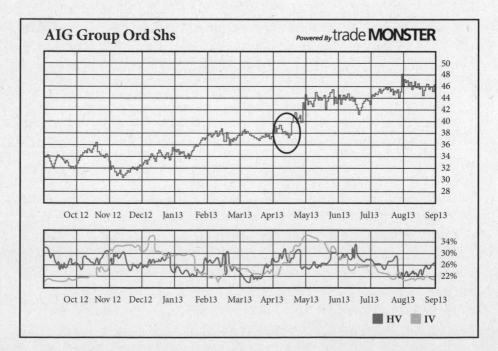

Time decay is the greatest in the front month, so in this case, with the stock at $38.50 and rising, we would sell one month out: May 37 puts for $1.05.

If the underlying price rises, and implied volatility drops (as was the case), it is best to buy back the put at some pre-determined value (say $.15).

As it happened, implied volatility held up for a couple of weeks before dropping to 24%. The stock price quickly rose above $41 and then $44. In this case, we were able to buy back the put for $.15 before expiration. This takes our profit off of the table and eliminates risk near expiration.

Example of a Losing Trade

Apple (AAPL) seemed to be putting a halt to its slide off the high in mid-October, while implied volatility spiked just before earnings. The price broke higher to $610 while the implied volatility was at 41, so we sold the December 600 put for $20.30.

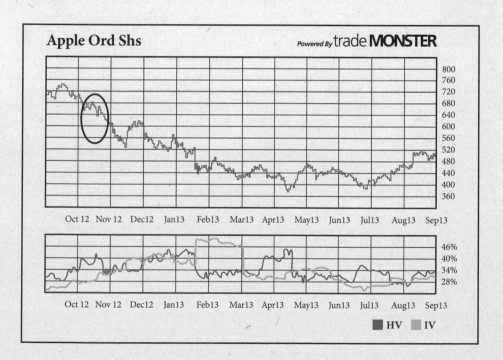

While implied volatility held constant, the price of the stock slid to $527 at expiration.

Now we had two alternatives. We could have bought back the put for a loss. Or we could have waited until expiration, if we were still bullish on AAPL and didn't mind buying it at $600.

Our break-even price at expiration was $579.70, so we would have bought this put back for a loss before the stock got as low as $527.

SUMMARY

- Short puts are a bullish to neutral strategy.

- They can generate extra income in your account.

- The risk is the same as owning the stock, minus the credit for selling the put.

- They can be a good way to acquire stock.

- They are equivalent to covered calls, but may offer some advantages.

- The maximum gain is capped, while the risk is the same as owning the stock.

VERTICAL SPREADS

Would you like to...
- Be able to increase your probability of profit?
- Reduce your exposure to high premiums and implied volatility?

One of the issues with buying "naked" calls and puts is that by the time you purchase them, the premiums are potentially already very high. As options trading is a probability game, the higher the premiums are, the lower the probability of profit for buyers. So to lower your exposure to those high premiums, you should know when to spread 'em.

Vertical Spreads are used to offset premium costs when buying options, or to hedge risks when selling options. The maximum gain and risk are known from the outset of the trade, and therefore allow for very specific risk management. Verticals are usually used when implied volatility, and therefore option premiums, is high.

What is a Vertical Spread?

Vertical spreads, a strategy done with either calls or puts, involve buying one option and selling another option of the same type and expiration, but a different strike.

A "bull call" spread, for example, entails buying one call and selling a higher-strike, lower-priced call to offset some of the premium cost. This type of spread would be done for a debit. A "bear call" spread would entail selling the lower-strike call and buying a higher-strike call to hedge the risk. This would produce a credit in your account; cash will be held as a margin for the position.

Debit vertical spreads (bull call and bear put spreads) profit from a directional move. The position will succeed if the stock has moved past the bought strike plus the debit paid. For a full profit, the underlying needs to move beyond the sold strike by expiration. For example, if XYZ call spread is purchased, buying the 25 call and selling the 30 call for a debit of $2, then the full profit will come with the underlying anywhere above $30, and the position will profit anywhere above $27.

Credit vertical spreads involving calls will make a full profit if the underlying is below the sold strike at expiration. The break-even is the strike plus the credit.

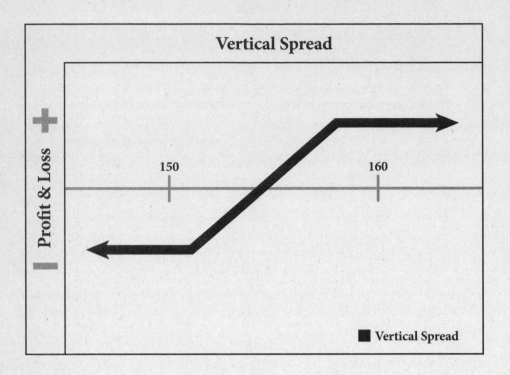

Vertical Spread

Profit & Loss

150

160

Vertical Spread

Credit spreads using puts will profit if the underlying stays above the strike sold minus the credit. Example: Sell the XYZ 30 put, buy the 25 put to hedge the risk, for a credit of 2.50. The position will profit anywhere above $27.50, and will get a full profit if XYZ is anywhere above $30 at expiration.

Vertical spreads lose if the underlying moves in the wrong direction. The maximum loss for debit spreads is the debit paid. The maximum loss for credit spreads is the difference between the two strikes used minus the credit. This is also the amount of margin held by your broker.

Debit vertical spreads are used to offset the premium cost of the purchased option, especially when implied volatilities are high. This increases the probability of profit for the trade, but does limit the potential gains. Credit spreads are used when one wants to be a net seller of options, but wants to hedge the risk. Option selling can have a very high probability of profit, but also the potential for large losses, and using a credit spread limits that exposure. With the stock at $149, the 150 call is purchased for $10, and to offset some of that cost, the 160 call is sold for $6, for a net debit of $4.

This is a directional trade, so the bull call spread will profit from the stock moving up and lose from the underlying moving down. The maximum gain and risk are known from the outset of the trade and therefore allow for very specific risk management. The spread is used to limit exposure to implied volatility, so changes in implied volatility will have little effect.

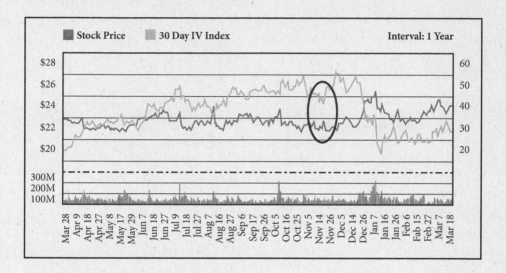

Example of a Winning Trade

Intel's (INTC) price puts in a higher low at the same time that implied volatility spikes on November 15. We usually look to call spreads on higher implied volatility to offset the premium cost.

With the stock at $21.50 and rising and implied volatility up to 27%, we would buy the May 22 calls for $.55 and sell the 23 calls for $.27, for a net debit of $.28.

The maximum risk is the $28 we paid (remember: the multiplier is 100 as one option is for 100 shares of stock) realized if the stock is below $23. The maximum gain is $73 if shares are above $23.

In this case, INTC went up to $24, so the trade worked out perfectly, giving us a 200% return.

Example of a Losing Trade

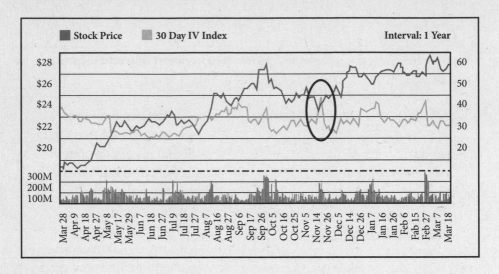

Here the price of the QQQ moved against our position.

In late October, we seemed to have the price bottoming out, with a spike in implied volatility. With the price at $65 and the implied volatility up to 21, we buy the 65 calls for $1.55 and sell the November 67 call for $.80. The net debit is $.75, which is our maximum risk.

The rebound doesn't happen, and the price dives down to $62 as the implied volatility holds steady. We would have sold the spread before expiration for $.35 given our risk rules and gotten out of the trade.

SUMMARY

- Vertical spreads provide known and fixed maximum gains and losses.

- They are usually used with high implied volatility and/or high premiums.

- They can be credit or debit spreads.

- They increase the probability of profit with directional trades, but limit the upside.

CALENDAR SPREADS

Would you like to...
- Be able to profit from range-bound markets?
- Take advantage of the different time decay rates in different expiration months?

Anyone who has traded options for a while has a feel for how time decay can eat away at an option's value, especially as expiration gets closer. Options positions can in fact profit from time decay, but this entails selling options and can involve significant risk. Long calendar spreads provide a limited-risk way to take advantage of time decay inherent in different expiration dates.

Long calendar spreads profit within a given range. They can also profit from a rise in implied volatility and are therefore a low-cost way of taking advantage of low implied volatility options. This is considered a more advanced options strategy, but usually has lower risk and a better probability of profit than outright call or put buying.

The maximum risk is known from the outset of the trade, and is equal to the debit paid for the spread, up until the near-month option that you sell gets to expiration, at which point exposure becomes the risk inherent in the option you bought.

What is a Calendar Spread?

Calendar spreads can be done with calls or puts and, if using the same strike, put and call calendar spreads are virtually equivalent. Implementing the strategy involves buying one option and selling another option of the same type and strike, but with different expiration. A long calendar spread would entail buying an option (not a "front month" contract) and selling a nearer-expiration option of the same strike and type. Long calendar spreads are traded for a debit, meaning you pay to open the overall position.

This strategy profits in a limited range around the strike used. The trade can be set up with a bullish, bearish or neutral bias. The greatest profit will come when the underlying is at the strike used at expiration. Calendar spreads also profit from a rise in implied volatility, since the long option has a higher vega than the short option.

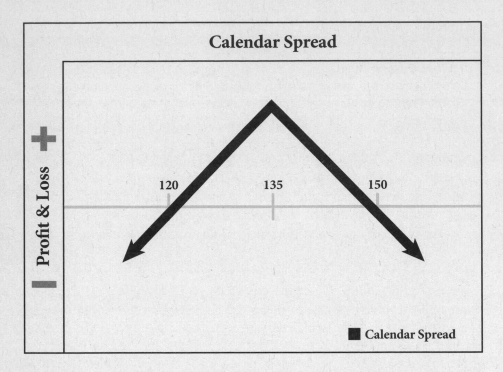

Calendar spreads lose if the underlying moves too far in either direction. The maximum loss is the debit paid, up until the option you sold expires. After that, you are long an option and your further risk is the entire value of that option.

Options in nearer-month expirations have more time decay than later months (they have a higher theta). The calendar spread profits from this difference in decay rates. This trade is best used when implied volatility is low and when there is implied volatility "skew" between the months used, specifically when the near-month sold has a higher implied volatility than the later-month bought.

In this example, with the stock at $135.13, the September 135 call is purchased for $15.45, and the July 135 call is sold for $10.45, for a net debit of $5, which is the maximum risk.

This is a neutral trade used when the outlook is for a range-bound underlying. The maximum risk is known from the outset of the trade, and is equal to the debit paid (until the first expiration). If the implied volatility does not change, the position profits from roughly $121 to $154. Rises in implied volatility will increase the profit and the range. Time decay is on your side with this trade.

Example of a Winning Trade

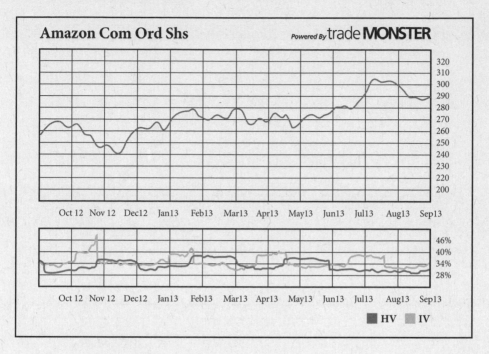

Amazon (AMZN) moved up to $271 in early March, while implied volatility pushed down to a 52 week low of 19%.

With the stock at $271, we would buy the May 270 calls for $9.50 and sell the April 270 calls for $7.30, for a net debit of $2.30.

The maximum risk is the $230 we paid (remembering that options contacts come in lots of 100). The risk would be realized if the stock moves "too far" in either direction.

In this case, AMZN was at $270 three days before that April expiration and at $260 at expiration. Implied volatility was up to 40. So the April 270 call expired worthless, while the May 270 call was worth $7.80, for a 200% return.

Example of a Losing Trade

Looking at Oracle (ORCL) charts, we see that establishing a spread before the March earnings would not have worked out. In early March, we saw the price hovering just below $35 and implied volatility around 25%. The May 25 call was

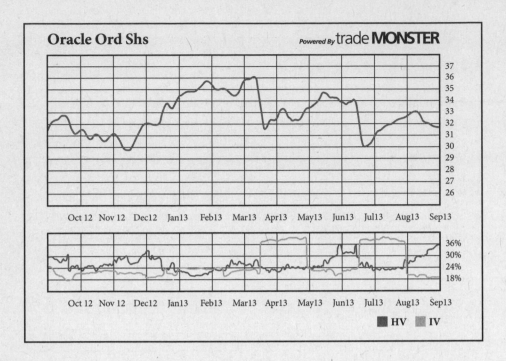

purchased for $1.55 and the April 35 call sold for $1.15, for a net debit of $.40. After earnings, the price plummeted down below $32 while implied volatility held steady. The April calls expired worthless, but given the price drop, the May calls were worth just $.15 at that time.

SUMMARY

- Calendar spreads provide known and fixed maximum loss up until the expiration of the short option.

- They are usually used with low implied volatility and the expectation of range-bound trade.

- Call calendars are virtually identical to put calendars, when using the same strike.

- They take advantage of the difference in time decay for different expirations

- They can be set up with a bullish or bearish bias.

DIAGONAL SPREADS

Why?

Long diagonal spreads are a form of calendar spread which combines a calendar spread with a vertical spread. They are used to take advantage of the difference in time decay between different expiration dates (the nearest month always has the most time decay), as well as taking a limited directional stance. The maximum risk is known from the outset of the trade until the near month option that you sold gets to expiration. Diagonal spreads can be done for a debit or a credit. If done for a debit, the maximum risk is the initial debit. If done for a credit, then there is a margin requirement similar to a credit vertical spread.

This is considered a more advanced options strategy, but usually has lower risk and a better probability of profit than outright call or put buying.

Diagonal spreads can be implemented using puts or calls and using the same strikes are virtually equivalent.

What?

Diagonal spreads can be done with calls or puts. Implementing the strategy involves buying one option and selling another option of the same type (call or put), but a different expiration and different strike. A long diagonal spread would entail buying an option (not the front month) and selling a nearer expiration option. An example would be buying the GOOG December 600 call and selling the GOOG September 560 call.

Diagonal spreads can be tailored to profit in a variety of ranges around the strike used. The trade can be set up with a bullish, bearish or neutral bias. The greatest profit will come if the underlying is at the sold strike at expiration. These also profit from a rise in implied volatility (the long option has a higher vega than the short option).

Diagonal spreads lose if the underlying moves too far from the strike sold. They are usually structured so that they will only produce a loss if the underlying moves too far in one direction (calendar spreads take a loss with a significant move in either direction).

Nearer-month expirations have more time decay than later months (they have a higher theta). The diagonal spread profits from this difference in decay rates. This trade is best used when implied volatility is low and when there is implied volatility skew between the months and strikes used (the option sold has a higher implied volatility than the option bought).

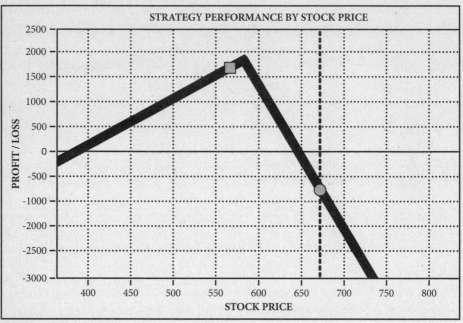

The theoretical risk profile of a diagonal spread

Example

With GOOG at $568.80, the September 620 call is purchased for $24.80, and the July 580 call is sold for $25.90. This is done for a credit of $1.10, but the margin requirement (cash required to hold the trade) is $38.90.

The initial profit/loss graph and credit/margin do not seem to make this an attractive trade. But time decay (theta) is a positive for this trade.

The trade has been structured to take a maximum profit if the price rises. A drop to the downside, regardless of how far, will produce some profit, while a significant rise will produce a loss.

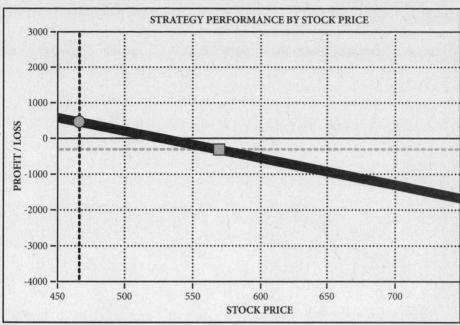

The risk profile at trade initiation

The spread profits from a rise in implied volatility, raising both the peak gain, as well as the upside break-even (increasing the price to which the price would have to rise to produce a loss). Time decay is on your side with this trade.

Winners

XYZ rallies to $108 in late February at the same time that volatility drops to below 50%. With the stock at $108 per share, the trader buys the April 125 calls for $1.50 and sells the March 120 calls for $1.70. The net credit is $0.20 per contract.

At March expiration, XYZ is trading at $119 per share, with volatility up to 65%. The March 120 call expires worthless, for a gain of $1.70, and the April 125 call is worth $2.25, a gain of $0.75. The net gain is $245 ($1.70 + $.75 = $2.45 X 100 contracts).

The trader now has the choice of closing the position and taking profits, or holding the long April 125 calls in the hopes the stock will continue to go up. This involves risk because volatility could fall and/or the stock could rise but not enough to put the April 125 calls in the money.

Losers

Before an earnings announcement, we see the price rallying up through $220 per share and volatility at 62%. The October 250 call is purchased for $9.60 and the September 240 call is sold for $7.90 – a net debit of $1.70 per contract. After the earnings announcement, the stock's price plummets down into the $80 range and implied volatility drops below 50%.

The volatility drifts upwards until the September expiration, when the short option goes out worthless. However, the stock's price has moved so far below the strike of the October calls that they too have lost virtually all of their value.

SUMMARY

- Diagonal spreads provide known and fixed maximum loss up until the expiration of the short option.

- They are usually used with low implied volatility and the expectation of range bound trade.

- They are usually hedged to one side (they will not produce a loss regardless of how far the market moves in one direction).

- Call calendars are virtually identical to put calendars at the same strike.

- They take advantage of the difference in implied volatility and time decay (theta) for different expirations and strikes.

BUTTERFLIES AND CONDORS

Would you like to...
• Be able to profit from range-bound markets?
• Take advantage of high option premiums?

Butterflies and Condors are trades intended to take advantage of a neutral outlook and/or high implied volatility. They involve selling two options and buying two options of different strikes around them, at a net debit. They establish a position which profits if the underlying stays within a given range.

The maximum risk and reward are known from the outset of the trade. The risk is equal to the debit paid for the trade and is incurred if the underlying moves too far in either direction. These strategies are considered more advanced because of the more complex construction. Essentially they combine two vertical spreads, one being a credit spread and the other a debit spread. Butterflies and condors have lower risk than call and put selling.

What are Butterflies and Condors?

Butterfly and Condor spreads can be done with calls or puts. Long butterflies using calls involve three strikes: you sell two calls at a middle strike and buy one call above and one call below that strike. Thus, you are combining a vertical bull call spread and a bear call spread with the short calls at the same strike.

Condors also combine a bull call spread with a bear call spread, but separate the sold calls by at least one increment. Condors have a wider range of profit, but cost more. Both spreads are done for a debit.

For example, a MSFT butterfly would entail buying a 27 call, selling two 28 calls, and buying a 29 call. A MSFT condor would involve buying a 26 call, selling a 27 call, selling a 28 call, and buying a 29 call.

Butterflies and condors profit in a limited range around the strikes of the options sold. The trade can be set up with a bullish, bearish, or neutral bias. The spread profits from a fall in implied volatility before expiration. Time decay is on your side, and increases profit. The greatest profit will come if at expiration the underlying is at the butterfly's short strike price, or anywhere between the two short strikes used for the condor.

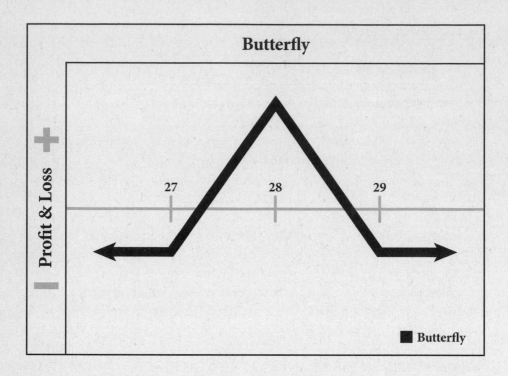

These spreads lose if the underlying moves too far in either direction. The maximum loss is the debit paid, and is incurred if the underlying moves beyond the strike of either of the long calls.

As an example, with the stock at $27.65, a trader could establish a butterfly by purchasing the a June 27 call and a June 29 call, while selling two June 28 calls, all for a net debit of $.25, which is the maximum risk. The maximum gain at expiration is $.75, if the price is right at $28

Example of a Winning Butterfly Trade

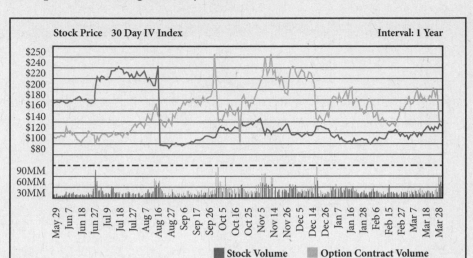

The stock and volatility rises but not the level of the short strike, so the position gains.

Let's say the above butterfly payoff diagram was bought for a net debit of $25: If Microsoft (MSFT) is $27.64 at expiration (that is, unchanged), the profit would be approximately $400.

If MSFT is at $28.75 or $27.25, the profit would be $0. These are the break-even points. The maximum risk is the $250 we paid, and would be realized if the stock is above $29 or below $27.

Example of a Losing Condor Trade

Now let's say we have bought the 26 call, sold the 27, sold the 28, and bought the 29 for a net debit of $.45.

If MSFT is between $27 and $28 at expiration, the maximum profit of $55 will be realized.

If MSFT is at $26.45 or $28.55, then the profit is $0 (break even). The maximum risk is the $45 paid, realized if the stock is above $29 or below $26.

SUMMARY

- Butterflies and Condors spreads provide known and fixed maximum gain and loss.

- They are usually used in cases of high implied volatility and expectations of range-bound underlyings.

- They can be implemented using puts or calls.

- Condors have a wider range of profit, but cost more.

- They take advantage of high implied volatility (seen as likely to fall) and time decay.

STRADDLES AND STRANGLES

Would you like to...
- Be able to profit from big moves—up or down?
- Take advantage of increasing volatility?

There are times when you just know that a big move in a stock is coming - the problem is that you don't know which direction. Wouldn't it be nice to have a strategy that could profit from such moves regardless if they were up or down?

Long "straddles" and "strangles" fit the bill. The strategies profit from volatility—sharp moves in the underlying, either up or down. They involve owning both calls and puts on the same underlying asset. These are some of the most expensive options strategies, but the maximum risk is known and fixed. Time decay and drops in implied volatility are the biggest threats to the strategy.

What are a Straddle and a Strangle?

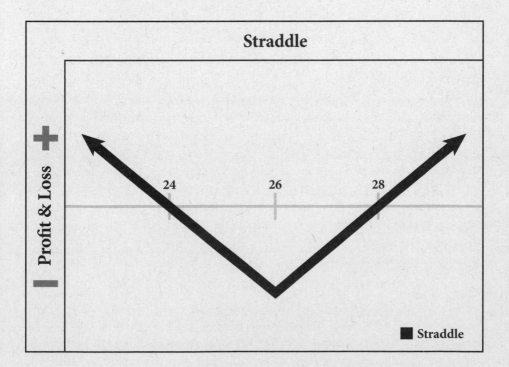

A straddle entails buying an at-the-money call and the same at-the-money put. The idea is that should the underlying significantly increase or significantly decrease, such that the new value of the call or the put can be sold for more than the cost to purchase the two positions, you profit.

A strangle takes the same approach, but uses an out-of-the-money call and an out-of-the-money put, to reduce the cost. This is a lower-cost trade, but requires an even greater move to be profitable.

Straddles and strangles profit from significant moves up or down in the underlying. A rise in the implied volatility will also increase the value of a straddle or strangle. Because you are paying two premiums, buying time value on both sides, the stock usually has to move considerably to produce big profits. Implementing the strategy simply involves buying a put and call with an expiration that gives the trade enough time to work, and straddle/strangle buyers are best served by not holding their positions as expiration gets close, as that is when time decay is greatest. Finally, the best time to buy options is when implied volatility is low.

This strategy loses if the stock price does not move enough to offset the time decay, or a fall in implied volatility. The maximum risk is the debit paid. If the implied volatility drops, the position can also lose value, even if the underlying moves. This is the reason that buying straddles or strangles before earnings (or other news) can be a risky strategy. Even if the stock moves, the drop in implied volatility that often happens after earnings are released can more than offset the gain from the move in the underlying.

This example uses a 26 straddle bought for $2.23, with the stock at $26.25. (Note that the option strike is unlikely to be exactly the same as the share price.) The position shows a profit if as expiration nears the stock price has moved beyond the strike prices used, plus or minus the debit paid to establish the call and put positions ($26 +/- $2.23).

The position will profit from significant moves up or down in the share price. The longer the move takes to happen, the bigger it needs to be, to offset time decay in the option price. Because implied volatility is a significant part of the premium paid for an option, if implied volatility goes down, the straddle will lose value and if implied volatility goes up, it will gain. This is only the case before expiration, because at expiration profit and loss is fixed.

Time is against you with a straddle or strangle. You have a position with significant negative theta and so every day you are losing value from time decay.

Example of a Winning Trade

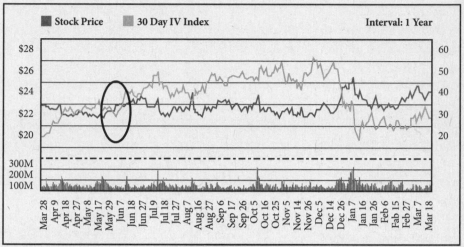

The negative effect of time decay

In the circled area, the price of Intel (INTC) bounces off a low while implied volatility stays low. Ideally we want to buy straddles on low implied volatility. Time decay is the opponent of the straddle and the greatest in the last month before expiration, so we need to give ourselves time to be right. In this case, with the stock climbing back above $23 and implied volatility at 30, we would buy three months out, choosing the August 23 straddle.

Within two weeks, the stock hit $24 and implied volatility went up to 40. The call tripled in value, while the put lost much of its value.

To exit the position, the straddle could have been sold in its entirety for a nice gain. When a position doubles in value, we generally consider closing half the position, so that no matter what happens next, we would break even.

Alternatively, the call could have been sold and the put held, in case there was a pullback. As can be seen, in fact the stock fell as low as $21 before the August expiration, meaning the put also would have given a 300% gain.

Example of a Losing Trade

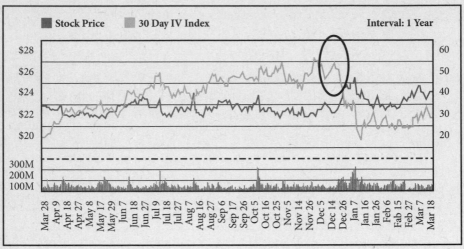

The negative effect of time decay

If we had bought a straddle a month earlier, the trade would not have worked out as well. Two things can go against us in buying straddles: implied volatility can go down, and time decay can eat away at the position.

In the highlighted area we see INTC breaking out to a new high. Enticed by current moves, many options traders ignore implied volatility and buy out-of-the-money options only in the near months.

So with the stock price at $27 and the implied volatility at 55, we would have bought the February 27 straddle.

The price did move up to $27.50, but with time decay and the drop in implied volatility, the position showed a loss. The price then fell and took the straddle value down to a 50% loss.

At that point, we would have exited the trade, since we generally consider that any position should be closed when it loses 50% of its value.

SUMMARY

- Straddles and strangles are delta-neutral, meaning we don't care if the price goes up or down, so long as it moves big in one direction or the other..

- They are a limited risk, but very expensive strategy.

- They are significantly affected by implied volatility and time decay.

- The maximum risk is limited; the maximum gain is theoretically unlimited.

BACKSPREADS

Why?

Backspreads are volatility trades that are used to take a directional, though hedged position. The position will have unlimited upside potential, but will also profit (if done for a credit) if the market stays flat or goes the wrong direction. The maximum risk is known from the outset of the trade and therefore allows for very specific risk management. The trade is a combination of a credit spread and long option.

This is considered a more advanced options strategy, but usually has lower risk and a better probability of profit than outright call or put buying.

What?

Backspreads can be done with calls or puts. Implementing the strategy involves selling an option and buying multiples of a of further out-of-the-money option of the same type and expiration, but a different strike. An example would be buying two 45 calls and selling one 40 call. This type of spread can be done for a debit, but most traders try to utilize backspreads when they can be done for a credit. Cash will be held as a margin for the position.

Backspreads are designed to profit from a strong direction move. Because the position is long more options than it is short, it will also profit from an increase in implied volatility. If done for a credit, the position will also profit if the stock price does not move, or even if it moves in the wrong direction.

Backspreads lose if the underlying moves up to the strike of the purchased options. The maximum loss occurs if the stock is at that strike at expiration, as the long options expire worthless and the short option also produces a loss. There is a margin held against the position.

Example

The risk profile of a call backspread is shown on the next page. With XYZ at $22.55, 2 of the 24 calls are bought for $.55 each and one of the 22 calls is sold for $1.45. The credit is $.35. The margin held is $2.00 – $.35 credit received, which is also the maximum risk ($22 - $24 = -$2.00 + $.35 = -$1.65).

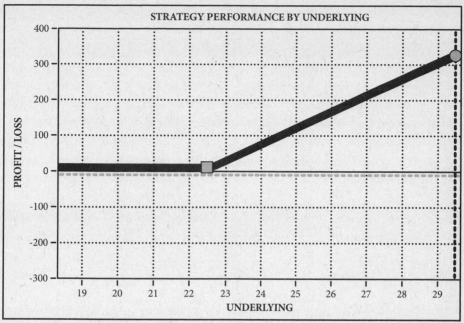

The risk profile at trade initiation

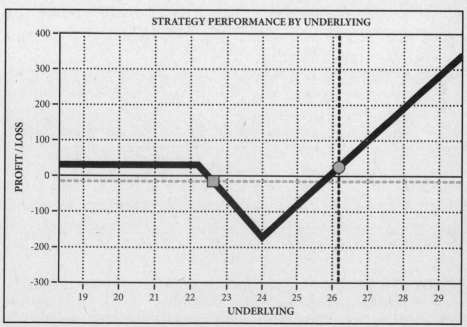

The theoretical risk profile of a backspread at expiration

Most traders will not hold the position until expiration, unless the price has dropped.

This is a directional trade, so the backspread will have the maximum profit from the stock moving up strongly. If the stock goes down the position is hedged and will still profit. The maximum loss occurs if the stock price moves up to the strike of the long options.

The position will profit from an increase in implied volatility up until expiration, when profit and loss is fixed.

Above the strike sold, time decay is against the trade. Below the strike sold (below $22), time decay is actually helpful.

Winners

XYZ price bounces off resistance at the same time that implied volatility spikes.

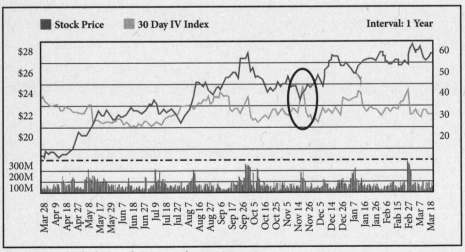

Using price and volatility together to spot a buying opportunity

With the stock at $23.50 and rising in mid-November, we will sell the December 22.50 call for $2.00 and buy two December 25 calls for $.85 for a net credit of $0.30. The maximum risk is $220, realized if the stock is at $25 at expiration.

In this case, XYZ went up to $26 fairly quickly enabling us to profit. Had the stock plummeted we still would have made $0.30 from the credit received when we put on the trade.

Losers

Had XYZ moved to $25 and stayed in that vicinity at expiration, the position would have produced a loss.

SUMMARY

- Backspreads profit from a strong directional move, but provide a hedge if wrong.

- They are usually used with low implied volatility.

- They are usually set up as credit spreads.

- They provide known and fixed maximum loss.

COLLARS

Why?

Collars provide protection for stock positions at low cost. This strategy is often used to lock in profits on an existing position. By combining a covered call with a protective put, both the upside and downside are capped.

The collar is constructed by being long stock + short out-of-the-money call + long out-of-the-money put in a 1-to-1-to-1 ratio. The collar is synthetically equivalent to the bull spread.

What?

Implementing the strategy involves buying or owning 100 shares of a stock and then selling a call that is "covered" by the stock and buying a put to protect the downside. The income from the call is used to purchase a lower strike put for protection. This can often be done for no cost, or even a credit, if the income from the sale of the call equals or outweighs the cost of the put. Selling the call does create the obligation to sell the stock if the call is assigned. This can create tax issues for stock with a low cost basis.

Collars profit up to, but not beyond the strike price sold. The maximum gain is realized if the stock price is right at, or above the strike price of the call sold. At that point the full value of the sold call is retained and the stock achieves its' maximum gain. For example: You sell a 50 strike call for $1 with the stock at 48. You use the credit to buy a 46 put, also for $1. You make money with any stock gains up to $50. The most you can make is $2 if the stock is at or above $50 at expiration.

The most you can lose is also $2, if the stock is anywhere below $46. The maximum loss occurs at the strike price of the purchased put. Below that level, the put will profit dollar for dollar with the stock and the loss remains constant.

A collar against stock is essentially identical to a vertical bull spread. The profit and loss is the same, but the amount of margin required is much larger for the collar. For this reason, the collar is usually applied to an already existing equity position to provide limited length downside protection. When considering a collar, it may also make sense to sell the stock and buy a vertical spread to reduce the margin requirement.

Examples

Here we see the risk profile of Apple with the stock at $184. A 200 strike call is first sold for $15 and a 170 put is purchased for $13.50. This is clearly a bullish position, and the position will rise and fall with the stock price, but not dollar for dollar.

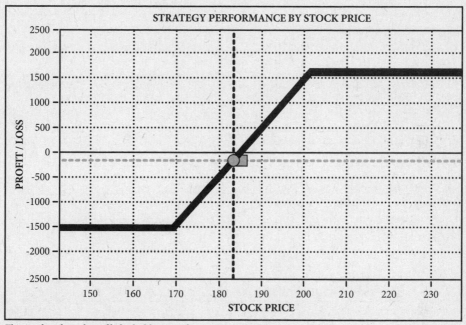

This is what the risk profile looks like at trade initiation

Detail

Clearly the position profits with a rise in the price of AAPL, but profits are limited up to the 200 strike, and assignment will happen above that. This position will profit if the stock does not move, as we have created a credit of $1.50. The maximum loss occurs at $170 and stays constant from there down.

The collar will perform just as the stock in the limited range between the strikes. The upside and downside are capped at those strikes.

Implied volatility has little effect, as you are both long and short an option and therefore have little to no exposure to changes in IV.

Time decay, as can be seen in comparing the above graphs, also has only a small effect, depending on whether the collar was put on for a credit (we benefit from time decay) or a debit (time decay is working against us).

Winners

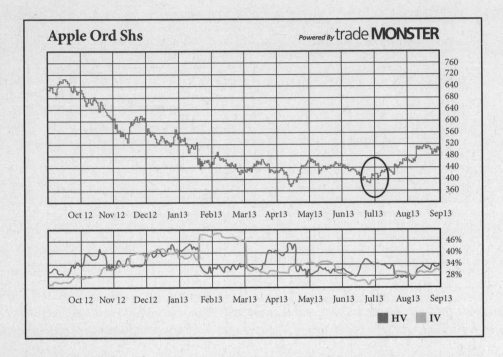

Apple Ord Shs   *Powered By* trade**MONSTER**

You purchased 1,000 AAPL shares at $400 as the stock rebounded off July lows. You put on a July collar, selling the 430 calls and buying the 370 puts for a credit of $.10. At July expiration, the stock finished at $424.95, producing a gain in the stock and allowing you to continue to hold the shares as the collar expires worthless.

On Monday after expiration, you put on another collar selling the 450 call and buying the 400 put for even money (the credit from the calls exactly equals the cost of the puts—a "no cost" collar). In this case, AAPL runs up through $450, all the way up to $500 by expiration. This is actually where a collar underperforms just owning stock. You have three choices in this case. You could buy back the short call as the stock climbs to it, you could roll up the collar, or you could hold the position, take the gains and lose the stock through the assignment of the short calls that are in-the-money.

Losers

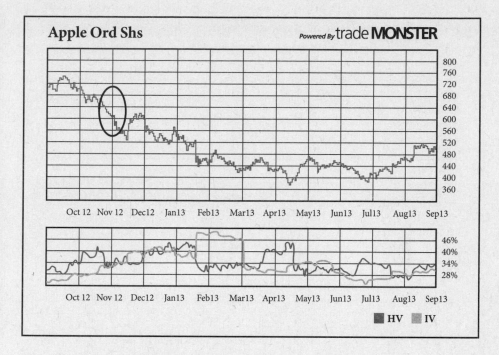

You purchased AAPL for $550 in November. You put on a collar in January to get through the end of the year, selling the $600 call, buying the $500 put for $1. The price drops right to $500 at expiration. The collar expires worthless, but you have the loss of $50 in the stock.

On Monday after expiration, you sell the 550 call, and buy the 450 put for even. The stock drops again, closing at $460. You lose another $40. This is the same as if you just owned the stock, but the protection you purchased had its own costs and did not even kick in as protection.

SUMMARY

- The collar involves owning or buying stock, selling out-of-the-money calls against it and buying out-of-the-money puts for protection. .

- It is a slightly bullish to neutral strategy.

- It is a low cost protective position.

- It is equivalent to a vertical bull spread.

- The maximum gain and loss are known and limited.

- The strategy can often be done for a credit.

OPTIONS PRICING

Option prices are derived from the Option Pricing Model. Along with the all-important theoretical value, the Option Pricing Model also provides us with a family of risk management tools known as the Greeks and, through some reverse engineering, the implied volatility. The model, although reasonably sophisticated in its math, is really just a probability model looking for an expected value (theoretical value). There are many different pricing models out there. The first was the Black Scholes model in 1973. Considered the grandfather of pricing models, Black Scholes won its creators the 1997 Nobel Prize in Economics.

Through the years, inadequacies in Black Scholes led to an evolution in option pricing models, making them much more accurate today. But, despite all the changes and adjustments that were made through the years, the factors or inputs to the model have mostly stayed the same. They are stock price, strike price, days to expiration, volatility, interest, and dividend. These factors combine to produce an option's theoretical value, incorporating both intrinsic and extrinsic value.

In this model, the stock price and the strike price work together to determine whether the option has any intrinsic value and how much value it may have. Meanwhile, the other factors, most notably volatility and days to expiration, combine to determine the amount of extrinsic value. Adding the intrinsic value and extrinsic value together, the total price of the option can be determined.

By knowing and understanding the inputs of the Option Pricing model, we can begin to understand how changes in these inputs will bring changes in the price of the option. A change in the stock price will obviously bring about a change in the price of the option. The amount of the price change that the option will see is described to us by a Greek known as delta.

Example: You buy an XYZ $65 call for $2.05 with the stock at $65.50. The stock trades up $2.00 to $67.50. The value of your call increases to $3.35.

When you first bought the call, the $2.05 consisted of $.50 of intrinsic value and $1.55 of extrinsic value. With the stock up $2.00 to $67.50, the value of your call (now $3.35) consists of $2.50 of intrinsic value and $.85 of extrinsic value. The option saw a small decrease in extrinsic value but an even larger increase in intrinsic value.

Now, this is where delta enters the picture. Since the increase in the option's price was $1.30 with the stock increasing $2.00, we can assume a delta of roughly 65. This is because the delta tells us how much the option's price will change per a $1.00 move. With this $2.00 move in the stock, we must divide by 2 to get the delta. It is important to note that delta only tells us the sensitivity of the options price to a movement in the underlying. It does not determine of the option's price.

More specifically, the stock price and strike price are the primary components in the intrinsic value of the option. Volatility and time are the major factors in the calculation to determine the extrinsic value of the option. This is why the model asks for a volatility assumption and the amount of days until expiration.

Options are considered a "wasting asset." This is not because options are considered to be a waste of money, but because options have a limited life. Options are limited in the fact that their life is limited. They have an expiry date.

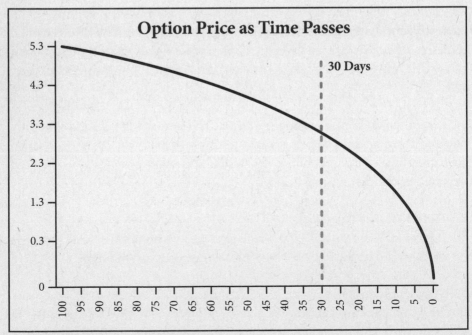

Accelerating time decay

Therefore, an options price is going to be susceptible to the passage of time. As time passes, an option's value decreases.

Example: With the stock at $65.50 and a volatility assumption of 30, the June 65 calls (with 18 days until expiration) are worth $2.05. At the same time, the July 65 calls (with 46 days until expiration) are worth $3.15 while the October 65 calls (with 137 days until expiration) are worth $5.25.

As you can see, all other things being equal, the more time that the option has until expiry, the higher the option's value. The intrinsic value of the option over time remains the same. June 65, July 65, and October 65 calls all have $.50 of intrinsic value. But, their prices are all different. This is due to the fact that time affects the option's extrinsic value. The more time that exists in the option, the more extrinsic value in the option and therefore the higher the option price.

Looking at this from the other side, the option will lose value as it gets closer to expiration, as the time to expiry decreases. This is where another Greek, theta, comes in. Theta tells us how much the option's extrinsic value decays per day.

The important thing we need to know about theta is that theta is non-linear. That means that the option's extrinsic value does not decay at the same rate through the life of the option. As we get closer to expiration, the daily decay rises on a daily basis. Like delta, it is important to note that theta is not a component of option pricing: days to expiration is. Theta simply shows us the sensitivity of the option's price to the passage of time from day to day.

Extrinsic value is also a product of volatility. The higher the volatility level is, the higher the amount of extrinsic value and thus the higher the option price. As volatility increases, the prices of all options increase. Vice versa, as volatility decreases, the price of all options decreases as the amount of extrinsic value in the options decreases.

Example: With the stock at $65.50 and a volatility assumption of 30, the June 65 calls are worth $2.05. If volatility were to increase 10 ticks to a level of 40 volatility, the price of the option would increase to $2.60.

As volatility increases, the expected range of the stock subsequently increases. That will increase the amount of extrinsic value due to the added uncertainty of which option will finish in-the-money and which options will not. Conversely, as the volatility level decreases, the amount of extrinsic value in options decreases, the price of all options decreases.

Another Greek, vega, tells us the sensitivity of the options price to the movement in volatility. Vega is given to us in cents. Vega tells us how much the option price will change with a one tick movement in volatility. When volatility increases, all option prices go up, and when volatility goes down, all option prices go down. Vega tells us how much. Keep in mind, like the other Greeks, vega does not determine an options price. Volatility does. Vega only tells us what the change in that price will be when the volatility assumption changes.

> **Example:** With the stock at $65.50, a volatility assumption of 30, and a vega of 0.05, the June 65 calls are worth $2.05. If volatility were to increase 1 tick to a level of 31 volatility, the price of the option would increase to $2.10. If volatility went up two ticks to 32, then the option price would go up $.10 to $2.15. If volatility went down, the mechanism would work the same way, but decreasing the price of the option.

Summary

- The price of an option is derived from the Option Pricing model.

- The factors that are entered into the model are stock price, strike price, days to expiration, volatility, interest, and dividend.

- The model also produces a family of risk management tools called the Greeks that measure the sensitivity of changes to the inputs of the model to the option.

THE GREEKS

Option prices can change due to directional price shifts in the underlying asset, changes in the implied volatility, the passage of time, and even changes in interest rates. Understanding and quantifying an option's sensitivity to these various factors is not only helpful — it can be the difference between boom and bust.

The option "Greeks" are a family of statistical references that identify and quantify an option's risk for an investor. Delta, gamma, theta, vega, and rho are generated from the Option Pricing model and are available to us prior to making a trade. This greatly aids the individual investor's risk management. Delta, gamma, theta, and vega are the Greeks that most concern option investors.

Delta

Delta measures the option's sensitivity to changes in the underlying stock price. It measures the expected price change of the option given a $1 change in the underlying. Using delta, investors can anticipate what the value of the option will be at a future given stock price. Delta can also be used to help determine the proper option to buy or sell under a specific situation. Calls have positive deltas and puts have negative deltas. For example, with the stock price of Oracle (ORCL) at $21.48, let's say the ORCL Feb 22.5 call has a delta of .35. If ORCL goes up one dollar to $22.48, the option price should increase by $.35.

The delta also measures the probability that an option will expire in-the-money. In the above example, the 22.5 call has a 35% probability of expiring in-the-money at expiration.

But note: Delta does not give us the probability that the stock price will be above the strike price any time during the options life, only at expiration.

Delta can be used to evaluate alternatives when buying options. At-the-money options have deltas of roughly .50. This is sensible, as statistically they have a 50% chance of going up or down.

Deep in-the-money options have very high deltas, and can be as high as 1.00, which means that they will essentially trade dollar for dollar with the stock. Some traders use these as stock substitutes, though there are different risks involved. Far out-of-the-money options have very low deltas and therefore change very little with a $1 move in the underlying. Factoring in commissions and the bid/ask spread, low delta options may not make a profit despite large moves in the underlying. Thus we see that comparing the delta to the option's price across different strikes is one way of measuring the potential returns on a trade.

Strike Price	June	July	October	January
50	100	99	94	90
55	100	95	85	81
60	91	81	72	70
65	56	56	57	58
70	18	30	41	46
75	3	13	28	35
80	0	4	18	26

Delta chart calls, 30 volatility, stock price $65.50

Strike Price	June	July	October	January
50	0	-1	-6	-10
55	0	-5	-15	-19
60	-9	-19	-28	-30
65	-44	-44	-43	-42
70	-72	-70	-59	-54
75	-97	-87	-72	-65
80	-100	-96	-82	-74

Delta chart puts, 30 volatility, stock price $65.50

Option sellers also can use the delta as a way to estimate the probability that they will be assigned. Covered call writers usually do not want to be assigned and so can use the delta to compare that probability with the potential return from selling the call.

Advanced traders often use "delta neutral" strategies, creating positions where the total delta is close to zero. The idea is two-fold. First, short option traders who are banking on lack of movement (stagnation) don't want to get caught leaning in one direction or the other. Second, investors who are expecting a large rapid movement in the stock (perhaps by result of an earnings announcement) but do not know which direction the stock may go, do not want to be leaning in the wrong direction when the movement occurs. Each approach carries risks, including the frequent adjustments necessary to remain delta neutral.

To review, delta is the option's sensitivity to the underlying price. The delta tells us how much an options price will change with a $1 move in the underlying. At-the-money options have a delta of roughly 50 and therefore will change roughly $.50 for every $1 change—up or down—in the underlying stock.

Gamma

As the stock moves, the delta of the option changes. Gamma measures the change in the delta for a $1 change in the underlying. Gamma is given to us in the amount of deltas. For instance, say you have a 60 delta call with a gamma of 3. If the stock were to trade up $1 then the delta would increase by 3 (the amount of gamma), creating a new delta of 63. If the stock had dropped $1 then the delta of your call would decrease by 3 (the amount of gamma), bringing it down to 57. Gamma works the same way for puts as it does for calls, except in the other direction.

Strike Price	June	July	October	January
50	0	.1	.7	.9
55	.1	.8	1.5	1.5
60	1.8	2.8	2.4	2.0
65	7.2	5.0	3.0	2.3
70	7.7	5.2	3.2	2.4
75	2.8	3.7	2.9	2.3
80	.4	1.8	2.3	2.1

Gamma chart, 30 volatility, stock price $65.50

Theta

Theta measures the option's sensitivity to the passage of time. It is a direct measure of the time decay of the option's extrinsic value. Theta is the given to us as a dollar amount of decay per day. This amount increases rapidly as expiration approaches because Theta is non-linear, meaning as the option approaches expiration the amount of decay increases on a daily basis.

Another characteristic of theta is that it is always highest at-the-money (ATM), and decreases as it moves away from the ATM option, in either direction. The greatest loss caused by time decay occurs in the last month of the option's life. The more theta you have, the more risk you have if the underlying price does not move in the direction that you want.

Strike Price	June	July	October	January
50	0	.007	.006	.005
55	.013	.013	.010	.007
60	.041	.033	.019	.011
65	.059	.042	.026	.018
70	.055	.038	.024	.016
75	.028	.024	.017	.009
80	.018	.020	.011	.006

Theta chart, 30 volatility, stock price $65.50

Option sellers use theta to their advantage, collecting time decay on a daily basis. The same is true of any strategy, including spreads, that produces a negative theta. Both vertical spreads and calendar spreads whose combined theta is negative are considered premium collectors. This means that with all other things being equal the passage of time will produce a profit. For instance, say we look at the June 40 calls worth $2.00 and having a .03 theta. The passage of one day will result in a decrease in the value of the call by $.03. So, the next day, the call will be worth $1.97. If you were long the call, you would experience a $.03 loss. If however, you were short the call, you would experience a $.03 gain.

Vega

Vega measures the option's sensitivity to changes in implied volatility. A rise in implied volatility creates a rise in option prices, and thus will increase the value of all the calls and puts. Vega is always highest ATM and decreases as it moves away from ATM in either direction. With each expiration (that is, further out in time), vega increases the amount of the extrinsic value of the option.

Strike Price	June	July	October	January
50	0	.001	.035	.080
55	0	.013	.076	.129
60	.011	.047	.123	.174
65	.050	.087	.156	.205
70	.053	.092	.164	.215
75	.018	.063	.149	.207
80	.003	.030	.120	.186

Vega chart, 30 volatility, stock price $65.50

Like theta, vega is given in dollar amounts. Vega will move the price of an option by that dollar amount per a one-tick movement in implied volatility. For example, the May 55 call is worth $3.00 at a 30 volatility. The option has $.05 vega. If implied volatility were to move up 1 tick to 31 volatility, the new value of the option would be $3.05. Conversely if implied volatility had dropped one tick from 30 to 29 then the new value of the May 55 call would be $2.95.

Rho

Rho is the option's sensitivity to changes in interest rates. Most traders have very little interest in this measurement. This is for two reasons. Interest rates play a very low weighted role in the Option Pricing model. Second, interest rates don't change very often and when they do it is in very small increments.

Using the Greeks to Buy an Option

Buying and selling stock is a relatively easy process. If you think the stock is going up, you buy the stock. If you think the stock is going down then you short the stock. But, when you decide to use options in place of the stock you bring a couple of other factors into the equation, namely time and volatility. These two additional factors are critical in determining the best strike and month to use to construct the strategy you determine to be optimal for the opportunity you identified.

Here lies the hidden value of the Greeks. As stated before, the main function of the Greeks is defensive, providing risk management analysis on your position. But here, the Greeks can also become offensive, providing you with information that helps you determine both optimal strategy and optimal construction of that strategy.

First and foremost, if the opportunity is a directional one, delta can play a major role. We know that delta tells us how much our option will change with a one-dollar movement in the stock. Delta really gives us an idea of mimicking power. A higher delta option will mimic the stock more closely than a lower delta option. So, if we want a strategy that is going to act like buying or selling the stock, then delta can help you zero in on the right option for your strategy.

Now, if you want to play an unsure direction, gamma can be of great value to you. As you remember, gamma tells you how much your delta changes with a one dollar movement in the stock. So, if you want to start acquiring delta to play a directional move when you don't know in which direction the movement will be, then an option with high gamma will provide a good sign as to which option will fit this situation.

When buying an option, we are obtaining both intrinsic and extrinsic value, the latter being susceptible to time decay. As an option buyer, this can be a disadvantage. But, if we knew where time decay is highest and lowest, we could do a good job in controlling our exposure to this daily decay of value. Many say you should never buy an option with less than 30 days until expiration; however, we know that theta is highest at-the-money and decreases as we move away from at-the-money in either direction. With this information, we can pick an option that fits our strategy and mitigates our decay risk at the same time.

As stated, when buying an option, we acquire extrinsic value that is affected by the passage of time (theta) in a negative way. But, the movement of implied volatility also affects the amount of extrinsic value and therefore must be accounted for and managed. Vega shows us which option will be more or less affected by the movement of implied volatility. If we decide that the specific opportunity we are looking at will most likely cause an increase in implied volatility then purchasing a higher vega option would be optimal. If you anticipate a decrease in implied volatility then the purchase of a lower vega option would be more appropriate.

SUMMARY

- The Greeks are risk measures that can help you choose which options to buy and which to sell. With options trading you must have an idea of the direction of the underlying as well as a view of the direction of implied volatility, and then factor in the timing of the potential opportunity.

- The Greeks can help you tailor your strategy to your outlook. Spreads, for instance, can help option buyers reduce theta and vega risk.

VOLATILITY

All options traders deal with volatility in every trade, whether they realize it or not. Volatility is a very important factor both in option pricing and the profitability of any trade. A call buyer is interested not only in the stock trading up, but in the stock going up enough to cover volatility's contribution to the option's extrinsic value. A covered call seller, to use another example, is betting that the stock does not move more than the amount of the extrinsic value which volatility contributes. So, to be a successful option trader, it is very important to understand volatility.

Types of Volatility

There are several types of volatility. The first is the actual volatility of the stock. This is called historic volatility or statistical volatility. Historical volatility measures the amount the stock moves over a one-year period. Although given as a yearly percentage, volatility can be measured over any time frame, allowing you to use it in any type of trading: day trading, swing trading, or even position trading.

Future volatility is the actual volatility of a forthcoming time period. Obviously, we can't know for certain what future volatility will be until after it becomes historic volatility, so we must venture an educated guess as to what future volatility will be. (This is a bit theoretical, but stick with us.)

Forecast volatility is the name for our private, educated guesses of what future volatility will be. Everyone has their own forecast volatility: It is to be different from person to person as everyone has their own opinion. This difference in the volatility assumption is the difference between being a buyer or a seller.

Implied volatility is the volatility expectation that is priced into every individual option. The implied volatility of an option is actually backed out of the pricing model. Being that all of the rest of the inputs of the options pricing model are known and the same to both parties, the only true variable is volatility. So, with that we can take any option price, plug it into the model as theoretical value and solve backwards for volatility. By doing this, we can determine the volatility of any option price. This is the option's volatility as implied by the model, hence implied volatility.

The importance of implied volatility cannot be understated. In the options world, relative value is not distinguished by total dollar amount. It can't be.

Different options have different strike prices and different expiration months so each option is like its own separate security. That would make comparisons between the two nearly impossible, like comparing apples to oranges. But, the level of implied volatility allows us to do this comparison. It enables us to decide which option is cheap and which is expensive. Implied volatility is factor that evaluates relative value in the option market.

As stated, volatility is a statistical percentage of a potential yearly stock movement encompassing one standard deviation. Thus, a stock with a higher volatility will have a wider range of potential stock prices over the course of a one-year period than a stock with a lower volatility.

> **Example:** If we have a stock trading at $100 with a volatility of 25%, the options are implying that the stock will be higher or lower by 25% within one standard deviation. (One standard deviation equals 68% in a normal distribution.) So the stock has a 68% probability of being between $75 and $125 in a one-year period.

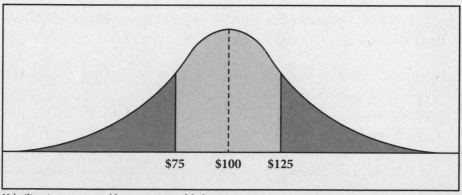

Volatility gives us reasonable expectations of daily price action

While the volatility data that we usually look at is an annual figure (the given number is a yearly percentage), you can also get monthly or daily numbers. The daily data can be obtained by dividing the volatility figure by the square root of the number of trading days in a year, which is usually accepted as 252. So if the volatility is 32%, the daily moves should be 2% (32 divided by the square root of 252, or approximately 16). That means that 68% of the time the daily moves should be 2% or less.

Volatility Charting

Most traders worry less about standard deviations and more about measuring the implied volatility of an option against past implied volatility and/or the historical volatility. This is where volatility charts are very useful, because they show the historical volatility against the average implied volatility.

Theoretically, the implied volatility for all options of a given underlying should be the same, but that isn't the case. So implied volatility averages can be used for given months or given time frames. This allows one to get a single number for implied volatility that can be charted. Often the 30-day average implied volatility is used, as is the case with the CBOE Volatility Index (VIX). Below is a chart of the 30-day historical volatility and the average implied volatility for the S&P 500 Index (SPX).

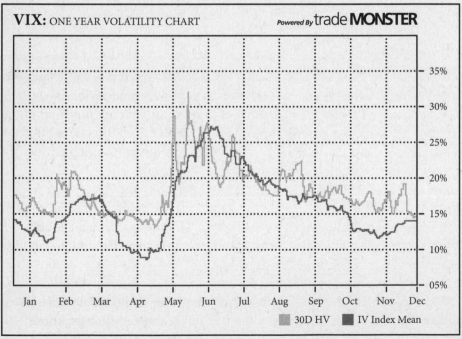

A look at the implied volatility of the S&P 500 Index

Valuing Options

There are several ways to use volatility data to value options. The basic premise is the same with volatility as it is for stocks: Buy low and sell high. The first is to simply compare the implied volatility to the historical volatility. Note that some stocks may have a historical volatility that is always (or near always) lower than the implied volatility of its options. If so, you may need to use a comparison (convergence/divergence) of the distance between the two.

The theory is that if the historical volatility is greater than the implied, then the option is cheap; if the historical is less than the implied, it is expensive. This can be done using the daily spot data, but that often presents an incomplete picture. As can be seen from the above chart, under this theory options appear expensive in early January but get much more expensive. And they appear cheap in late February and early March but get much cheaper.

Volatility charts allow traders to do more thorough analysis. Comparing the implied volatility of an option to past implied volatility and historical volatility allows for trades with higher probability of success.

Appropriate Strategies

Many option traders focus specifically on volatility. The thesis that changes in volatility are much easier to predict than changes in the underlying asset prices has attracted a lot of academic interest. Volatility is, after all, mean-reverting and bounded both to the upside and downside. But even directional traders, who only want to use calls and puts for leverage or protection, can benefit greatly from a basic knowledge of volatility.

Volatility is a relative measure. Having a volatility number means nothing without knowing the average or mean volatility of the asset you are looking at. With a mean volatility, we can now identify what is considered high volatility and what is low volatility.

When the implied volatility is low, it's a good time to buy an option. When implied volatility is high, it can be a good time to sell or use a spread strategy. Those who stick with directional trades are best served by using call or put spreads when implied volatilities are high. Those using covered calls are best served selling calls when they are relatively "overpriced" from a standpoint of volatility.

It is important to know how implied volatility can react to upcoming events. The implied volatility often gets inflated leading up to news releases or earnings announcements. After the news is out—when the unknown becomes known, implied volatility tends to drop sharply. This is the reason that many traders who have bought an option before such an announcement, and been right on the direction, still lose money. The money made by choosing the right direction in the stock was overwhelmed by the decrease in volatility.

The following chart shows how implied volatility (the light gray line) gets inflated and deflated around earnings announcements (the darker gray line is the 30-day historical volatility).

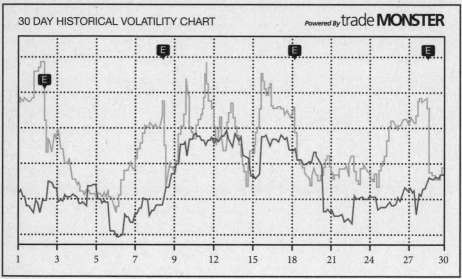

The divergence of implied and historical volatility

SUMMARY

- Historical volatility is a measure of how much the underlying asset has been moving in the past.

- Implied volatility is a function of an option's price and is backed out of the Option Pricing Model.

- Implied volatility shows the expectation of future volatility.

- Volatility charts one standard deviation, usually on an annual basis.

- Volatility charts are invaluable for getting an idea of the relative value of an option.

- Using both historical and implied volatility is helpful.

ACKNOWLEDGEMENTS

"How We Trade Options" reflects a lifetime of trading, learning, and friendships. No other profession so clearly demonstrates that while our mistakes are our own, our successes create debts of gratitude.

We would like to acknowledge all our peers on the floor, upstairs and down, as well as the hedge fund traders and institutional brokers who understand how difficult it is to take complicated financial topics and make them understandable to those not in the business. We're always grateful for your comments and critiques.

We also extend our thanks to Mark Hoffman and Nikhil Deogun, who uphold CNBC's standard as being the top financial network and a great place to work. To John Melloy, Lydia Thew, Melissa Lee, and Scott Wapner, who set the stage for great shows and do fabulous work on both sides of the camera. To all the wonderful women in the Makeup Department, because we understand that our bald heads take twice as much time and product, yet somehow you manage to work miracles daily. And to our fellow traders on "Fast Money": You men and women are smart, fun, and always work hard to make our shows the best they can be.

We'd be remiss if we didn't thank the great, dedicated people at the NYSE, NASDAQ, CBOE, and CME who support our work, allow us to broadcast from their trading floors, and make our time there as comfortable as possible.

We must acknowledge each one of the tradeMONSTER Group's shareholders. As we have grown our businesses, you guys have been behind us 100 percent. Your vision and support have been vital to the success of optionMONSTER and tradeMONSTER: Without you, this would not have been possible.

We also thank our optionMONSTER team, led by Dirk Mueller and Kurt Oeler, and other key staff members, including Mike Yamamoto, David Russell, Chris McKhann, and Ron Ianieri. You've never lost focus even though the road has not been easy. It's taken strong will and dedication to do what you guys have done, but you did it and continue to keep us moving in the right direction. And to our social media guru Andrew Coffey, who is always in pursuit of the next new thing and makes sure we stay ahead of the pack.

We'd like to recognize the vast majority of people in financial markets who are extremely ethical, have high morals, and fight for what's right. To those who take the opposite tack, we hope you know the third and fourth circles of Hell await!

Lastly, we'd like to acknowledge the fans who encourage us every day. We can't express how valuable this is to our mental health (not to mention our egos!). It's wonderful that so many of you reach out to us via Twitter, Facebook, at our conferences, or outside the studio in Times Square. Thank you all!

NOTES

NOTES

NOTES

NOTES

NOTES

NOTES

NOTES

NOTES

NOTES

NOTES

NOTES

NOTES